Building a
WORDPRESS
BLOG
People Want to Read

SCOTT McNULTY

Building a WordPress Blog People Want to Read

Scott McNulty

Peachpit Press
1249 Eighth Street
Berkeley, CA 94710
510/524-2178
510/524-2221 (fax)

Find us on the Web at: www.peachpit.com
To report errors, please send a note to errata@peachpit.com

Peachpit Press is a division of Pearson Education.
Copyright © 2009 by Scott McNulty

Executive editor: Clifford Colby
Editor: Kathy Simpson
Production editor: Danielle Foster
Compositor: WolfsonDesign
Indexer: Julie Bess
Cover design: Charlene Charles-Will
Interior design: WolfsonDesign

ISBN-13 978-0-321-59193-7
ISBN-10 0-321-59193-3

9 8 7 6 5 4 3 2

Printed and bound in the United States of America

Blogging has brought a tremendous number of fantastic things into my life, but none better than my lovely girlfriend, Marisa. This book is dedicated to Marisa for her patience and support throughout the process of writing the book. I think she might be a keeper.

About the Author

Scott McNulty is a simple geek living in Philadelphia. Scott has been blogging for just over nine years about whatever strikes his fancy. He runs more WordPress blogs than anyone should and even has a few other blogs using other blogging engines.

More of Scott's words can be found in his personal blog, blog.blankbaby.com; at MacUser.com, where he is a senior contributor; and at Obsessable.com, where he writes a weekly feature about technology.

Acknowledgments

Lots of smart and talented people worked very hard to make me look good, which is a Herculean task. Thanks to Cliff Colby for making this book happen; to Kathy Simpson for making sure my words were intelligible (any garbled or wrong sections of this book are entirely my responsibility); and the production team of Danielle Foster, WolfsonDesign, and Julie Bess for their help in making a book that I'm darned proud of.

I'd also like to thank my bosses, Joe Cruz and Dan Alig, for being so flexible with my work schedule as I wrote this book. Not all workplaces would be so accommodating, and I'm thankful that I work in such an enlightened place.

Contents

Chapter 7: Publishing Your Post (Finally!)..... 127

Chapter 8: Working with Pages 147

Chapter 9: Handling Links 157

Chapter 10: Coping with Comments 173

1

Why WordPress?

Everyone from Martha Stewart to Fortune 500 companies to your 12-year-old niece seems to be blogging nowadays. Blogging has gone from something only the nerdly found themselves doing a few years ago to something that your mother likely knows about—if she isn't doing it herself.

WordPress has done its part to help spread the allure of blogging by making it very easy to start a blog—and to update that blog after it's up and running. WordPress isn't the only blogging tool in town. Lots of popular tools are out there, including Movable Type, Tumblr, Habari, and Blogger. Given all these choices, why should you use WordPress?

Check the following sections for the good and the bad about WordPress. To get it out of the way, I start with the bad.

The Downside of WordPress

All is not sunshine and fruit punch in the world of WordPress. Using a blogging platform that is engineered like this one has a couple of drawbacks:

- **Appeal to bad guys.** Popularity and an open codebase are generally a good combination, but a few people out there are always looking to ruin everyone's fun. Because WordPress runs so many high-profile sites, some nefarious types are on the lookout for flaws that can be exploited. Luckily, the WordPress developers are very quick to patch vulnerabilities, but you have to stay on top of the releases.

- **Dynamic page generation.** WordPress dynamically generates most of the pages that you see. Each time you load a post, a bunch of things are happening in the background: Database queries are fired off, PHP code is executed, and then the page is displayed. Usually, this system isn't a problem; it ensures that the content of your blog is as up to date as possible. But this approach is a little more resource intensive than a static approach and can translate to your blog's being unavailable under heavy load.

note Movable Type, the other blogging heavyweight, takes the opposite approach. Movable Type (MT for short) stores posts, comments, and the like in a database just like WordPress does, but it creates static HTML pages from that data. This arrangement makes MT a little leaner when serving up content, but publishing a post can take more time because each index page needs to be rebuilt. MT has added an option to use a dynamic system, but by default, it publishes static pages.

The Upside of WordPress

Remember when you were a kid, and you asked your mom if you could do something all the other kids were doing? She replied, "If everyone else jumped off a bridge, would you jump off too?" Despite the fact that my friends weren't known bridge-jumpers, the advice is clear: Be your own person, and you'll be better off in life.

That advice works well as a general life practice, but when you're considering a blogging platform, you want to pick the one that has the most users. Why? Because along with all those users comes some pretty neat stuff, such as an active developer community, a wide range of reference materials, and a large base of people you can turn to for help.

WordPress has all those features in spades. Many of today's most popular blogs—including TechCrunch, ICanHasCheezburger.com, and *The New York Times'* blogs—are powered by WordPress, so you can rest assured that WordPress is capable of handling the traffic generated by your adoring audience.

Furthermore, WordPress can be extended by little bits of code called *plug-ins,* which I talk about in detail in Chapter 13. Created by members of the WordPress community, plug-ins are often available for free or for a small fee. These plug-ins can make WordPress do all sorts of things it isn't able to do out of the box.

The active plug-in developer community owes its existence in large part to the fact that WordPress is distributed under the GNU General Public License. This license means two things:

- WordPress is free.

- You're allowed to alter the code to suit your needs and share your modified code with anyone, so long as you distribute it under the same license (for free and in such a way that others can change your code and share it as well).

WordPress.com vs. WordPress.org

Now that I've convinced you that WordPress is the way to go, you have another choice to make: self-hosting or hosted version?

Hosting your blog on WordPress.com

WordPress.com (**Figure 1.1**) hosts WordPress blogs for free. Hosting your blog on WordPress.com frees you from having to get your own hosting space and making sure that your Web server has the software that WordPress needs to run. It also means that your blog is ready for traffic spikes associated with popular posts. The team behind WordPress.com takes care of all the back-end stuff (patching servers, upgrading software, and the like) and leaves the blogging to you.

Figure 1.1 The WordPress.com logo.

Keep a few things in mind when you host your blog on WordPress.com:

- **WordPress URL.** The URL of your blog will be something like www.*mygreatblog*.wordpress.com. If you're going to host a blog for professional reasons, you may not want to advertise the fact that you're using a free service.

- **Extra cost for advanced features.** WordPress.com offers some advanced features such as domain mapping, which allows you to point any domain to a blog hosted on WordPress.com (getting around the amateurish URL), but you have to pay for these features.

- **No access to code.** Given the nature of WordPress.com, you have no access to your blog's code. You can't modify the way your theme looks without paying a little extra, and you can't upload your own custom theme.

    Remember those cool plug-ins I mention earlier in this chapter? WordPress.com offers a bunch of them for your use, but you can't upload your own plug-ins, so if you're interested in using one that isn't available on WordPress.com, you're out of luck.

note   You can use your own plug-ins when you buy a VIP WordPress.com package, which starts at $600 a month. If this blog is your first one, however, I don't recommend going that route.

WordPress.com is a great option if you're looking to get into blogging with WordPress but don't want to make a big commitment. Registering is free and easy, and you'll be up and blogging in no time.

This book concentrates on the other option: hosting your own installation of WordPress. That being said, much of the content of this book (especially the chapters about posts, pages, and links) are valid for both blogs hosted on WordPress.com and self-hosted blogs.

Hosting your own installation of WordPress

Your other option is downloading the WordPress code from WordPress.org (**Figure 1.2**) and installing it yourself. Because you're hosting the blog yourself, you decide what plug-ins you'll use, and you have complete control of all the files. What's more, pointing a domain to your installation won't cost you anything extra (above and beyond your Web-hosting bill and registration fees, that is).

Figure 1.2 The WordPress.org logo.

This option gives you the most control of your blog, but it does come at a price: You're responsible for everything. You have to maintain backups of your blog and make sure that your blog is ready for a sudden surge in traffic, and you won't have anyone but yourself to blame if you screw something up.

Hosting your own installation of WordPress won't be much of a challenge if you've maintained a Web site before. If you're new to Web hosting, you'll have a learning curve (but you have this book to help you!).

2

Installing WordPress

The famed 5-minute installation is one of the most-talked-about aspects of WordPress. I've installed WordPress several times (a good thing, because I'm writing a book about it), and the process has always been painless, but knowing a few things will make it much smoother for those who are new to WordPress.

The most common way to install WordPress involves using a remote *server*—a computer that's set up to serve Web sites to anyone who wants to visit them. I concentrate on this option for most of the book.

You can also do what is known as a *local install* of WordPress by using your own computer as a local server. This installation isn't accessible to other folks but is good for testing. I won't be covering local installs in this book, however.

Getting What You Need

In this chapter, I walk you through installing WordPress on a remote server. First, though, you need to gather some files and tools, and double-check some settings. WordPress requires certain programs to be available on your remote server, and to access that remote server from your computer, you need an FTP client.

A Web host

You need to have Web-hosting space before you can install WordPress. Picking a hosting company is a topic that could be a book in and of itself. But here are a few things to look for in a host, because your host has to have them for you to run WordPress:

- **PHP version 4.3 or later.** WordPress itself is written in PHP, so it makes sense that PHP has to be installed on the server for WordPress to run.

- **MySQL version 4.0 or later.** MySQL is an open-source database that stores all sorts of information for your WordPress install. All your posts, users, and settings will be stored in this database. (I cover setting up the MySQL database later in the chapter.)

Local tools

When your Web hosting is all set, you need to make sure that you have the necessary tools on your local machine to set up WordPress. Here's the list:

- **FTP client.** You need to get files from your computer to your hosting space. You have several ways to transfer files, but the easiest is *FTP* (geek talk for *File Transfer Protocol*). FTP isn't a program, but an agreed-upon protocol that programs use to transfer files. File-transfer programs that use the FTP protocol—called *FTP clients*—are available for every operating system. For more information, see the nearby "FTP Clients" sidebar.

- **A text editor.** The WordPress application is made up of files that you can edit with any plain old text editor. (Windows users can use Notepad, for example; Mac OS X users can use TextEdit.) Before you use your FTP client to upload files to your hosting space, you need to use a text editor to edit a configuration file (see "Editing the wp-config File" later in this chapter).

note Any text editor will do the trick, but don't use Microsoft Word. Word adds a bunch of stuff to text files that only causes trouble with WordPress files.

FTP Clients

Chances are that you're using either of two operating systems (OSes) on your computer: Apple's Mac OS X or a flavor of Microsoft Windows. Both OSes have command-line FTP tools built into them, but I'm a graphical-interface kind of guy. Here are some FTP clients that you should check out.

For Windows:

- **FileZilla.** FileZilla (http://filezilla-project.org/) is free; open source; and available for Windows, Mac, and Linux computers. You can't beat that!

- **WS_FTP.** WS_FTP (www.ipswitchft.com/) has been around forever. Both the Home and Professional versions are feature packed—as they should be, because pricing starts at $39.95 for the Home version.

For Mac OS X (my OS of choice):

- **CyberDuck.** CyberDuck (http://cyberduck.ch/) is open source and full featured. And who doesn't like ducks?

- **Transmit.** Transmit (www.panic.com/transmit/) is the gold standard of FTP clients for the Mac and is made by a great indie Mac developer (Panic). For $29.95, you get one license for this well-thought-out FTP client.

The WordPress code

After you've gathered all your tools, you need the raw materials: the WordPress files. Getting these files couldn't be easier. Simply point your browser to www.wordpress.org/download. You'll see an orange box with a large link for downloading the most current and stable version of WordPress, which is WordPress 2.6.2 at this writing (**Figure 2.1**).

Figure 2.1 The WordPress download page. See that big orange box? That's where you can snag your own copy of the WordPress code.

Notice that I said the orange box links to the *stable* version of WordPress. If you like living on the edge, you can check out the Beta Releases and Nightly Builds links on the left side of the page.

Beta Releases

The word *beta* should be familiar to anyone who's used the Web in the past few years. A *beta release* of a product allows the public to use that product before it's fully done. When you use a beta release, you get in on the snazzy new features ahead of the rest of the population, and the company gets an unpaid tester to encounter any nasty bugs that may be lurking in the not-ready-for-prime-time code.

What Are Those Files, Anyway?

You've downloaded and uncompressed the latest version of WordPress, and now you have a folder called wordpress sitting on your computer. A quick peek inside the folder reveals a bunch of other files and folders. Not too impressive, is it?

Sorry if you were expecting more, but that handful of files is going to enable you to share your thoughts (and cat pictures) with the entire world. That's pretty powerful stuff, wouldn't you say?

At this point, you can ignore most of the files in the wordpress folder. You may want to check out the read-me file (though this book is far more entertaining), and if you're curious you can open any of the files in your favorite text editor. Just make sure not to change any of the code, because changes could lead to unexpected behavior in your install.

You can join the WordPress beta program by signing up on the tester list—but if you're new to WordPress, you shouldn't sign up unless you're a fan of the "sink or swim" learning methodology.

Nightly Builds

Nightly builds often are even scarier than betas. WordPress is a large open-source project, which means that an army of people out there are using their free time to work on the code that powers WordPress. When a creator is done with the code, he or she checks it into the system for someone else to look over. After all the changes have been given a once-over, a *nightly build* is created, containing all the most recent, untested changes.

I suggest downloading a nightly build of WordPress only if you're the type of person who has to be on the bleeding edge. If you buy your cell phone from eBay Japan just so you can have it a few weeks before your friends, the nightlies may be up your alley.

WordPress.org maintains an archive of old WP releases, just in case you're hankering for some olde-tyme WordPress. Point your browser to http://wordpress.org/download/release-archive/ for a trip down memory lane. Be warned, however, that many of these releases were superseded by new releases that fixed security issues. Download at your own risk.

Setting up the MySQL Database

It's almost time to install WordPress, but first, you need to create a MySQL database for WordPress to store all your content and user accounts. The installation will fail if you don't set this database up beforehand.

Delving into the ins and outs of setting up a MySQL database is beyond the scope of this book, but here are some pointers:

- Name your database something that you'll remember.

- You'll need to create a database user that will install all the WordPress tables (the install script takes care of this process). Don't use the same user name and password that you're going to blog with; using a different name and password makes it a little harder for folks to guess your database credentials.

 The database user who installs WordPress needs to have full rights over the WordPress database, meaning that the user can create— and delete—all manner of things. A good password is your best defense against malicious tomfoolery.

Editing the wp-config File

 This section, like the rest of the book, assumes that you're using WordPress 2.6. Most of the information will be valid for older versions (and, I hope, for future versions), but you may notice some differences if you aren't using WordPress 2.6.

Now that all the prep work is done, you're ready to get your hands messy with a little WordPress code. If you're code squeamish, worry not! The file you're about to look at is honest-to-goodness PHP code, but I'm here to help you. (Also, the bits you're interested in for purposes of WordPress are well documented in the code itself.)

Look inside the wordpress folder on your computer, and open the file called wp-config-sample.php (which I'll call *wp-config* for short). You should see a bunch of code, along with some very helpful comments about what you should, and shouldn't, touch in this file.

The wp-config file has four sections, which I'll call MySQL Settings, KEY, Languages, and "not for editing."

MySQL Settings

The MySQL Settings section is how WordPress knows where to look for the MySQL database you set up earlier. All you need to do is enter some information in this file.

 note   **Remember to enter all your values between quotation marks; otherwise, your install will fail.**

Here's the text of this section:

```
// ** MySQL settings ** //
define('DB_NAME', 'putyourdbnamehere');
  // The name of the database
define('DB_USER', 'usernamehere');
  // Your MySQL username
define('DB_PASSWORD', 'yourpasswordhere');
  // ...and password
define('DB_HOST', 'localhost');
  // 99% chance you won't need to change this value
define('DB_CHARSET', 'utf8');
define('DB_COLLATE', '');
```

And here's what you need to fill in:

- DB_NAME is the name of your database. (I usually call my databases something creative like *blogname*-wp, where *blogname* is the name of the blog that I'm installing.)

- DB_USER and DB_PASSWORD are where you enter the user name and password of the MySQL database that you created.

- DB_HOST is the name of the computer that is running your MySQL database. More often than not, you can leave this variable set to 'localhost', which means that the database is running on the same machine that hosts your WordPress install. If your blog is hosted on a larger Web host, however, check the host site's documentation for the proper value.

- DB_CHARSET and DB_COLLATE both have to do with the character set that your MySQL database is using. If you have no idea what that sentence means, you should leave these variables set to the defaults.

One database setting in the default wp-config file isn't grouped with the others, but it's very important if you plan to point multiple WordPress installs to one MySQL database. $table_prefix allows you to set a custom table prefix for each WordPress install. The default prefix is wp_, which means that every table created by the install will have wp_ as its first three characters. This arrangement is fine if you plan to have only one WordPress install per MySQL database, but if you want to use one database for more than one blog, you need to set a custom prefix for each blog. (Otherwise, every installation would create exactly the same tables, overwriting what was already there and making you lose data, which is never fun.)

KEY

Here's the text of the KEY section:

```
define('AUTH_KEY', 'put your unique phrase here');
   // Change this to a unique phrase.
define('SECURE_AUTH_KEY', 'put your unique phrase here');
   // Change this to a unique phrase.
define('LOGGED_IN_KEY', 'put your unique phrase here');
   // Change this to a unique phrase.
```

The KEY section is all about making your installation of WordPress more secure. You may be tempted to skip this section because it's optional (WordPress will work just fine if you don't assign three unique key values here), but it's such a great way to secure your blog that it's well worth a few seconds of your time.

What do these keys do? WordPress uses *cookies*—little files that are stored in your Web browser to remember who you are and what your login information is. A hacker could grab one of your cookies (no one likes to share cookies!) and log into your blog posing as you. Setting these keys lets WordPress *hash* (scramble) those values to make it much harder for someone to get any information from the cookies. (He'd need to guess your hash key to unscramble the values, which is why the keys should be very complex.) These keys are also used in your MySQL database to make the passwords stored there harder to decipher.

The keys work best when they're completely random and more than 60 characters long. I have two pieces of good news that will make using these keys seem much more attractive:

1. You never have to remember the values of these keys. You set them once in your wp-config file and then forget about them (though they'll be stored in the file itself, should you feel nostalgic for them).

2. The smart folks behind WordPress set up a service that generates three very strong, and very random, keys for you. All you have to do is visit http://api.wordpress.org/secret-key/1.1/, which generates the code for you; just copy and paste that code into your wp-config file. Nothing could be easier.

Seriously, stop reading these instructions and set those keys. I'll wait.

Done? Good! I'll move on.

Languages

The default WordPress language is English, which is great for us English-speaking bloggers. But what if you want to blog in another language? That's where `define ('WPLANG', '');` comes in.

Localizing WordPress to another language requires a few steps:

1. Define WPLANG to the language code you want.

2. Create a folder called languages inside the wp-content folder of your WordPress installation folder.

3. Obtain the proper MO file for the desired language, and put it in your new language folder.

   The MO file contains all the information that WordPress needs to be displayed in anything from Italian to Portuguese. Volunteers create these files, some of which are available here: http://codex.wordpress. org/WordPress_in_Your_Language. You can also find a full list of the codes needed to define the WPLANG variable to your language of choice.

"Not for editing" section

Astute readers will note that I didn't mention the final section of the wp-config file:

```
if ( !defined('ABSPATH') )
  define('ABSPATH', dirname(__FILE__) . '/');
require_once(ABSPATH . 'wp-settings.php');
```

I have a very good explanation for this omission: You shouldn't edit that part of the file. The wp-config file acts as a repository for settings that another file—wp-settings.php—uses to do all the heavy lifting of the WordPress installation. Fiddling with this section of the file will result in installation errors, so don't touch it!

Example wp-config file

Here's an example wp-config file all filled out:

```
<?php
// ** MySQL settings ** //
define('DB_NAME', 'wpforall');     // The name of the database
define('DB_USER', 'wpforalldb');      // Your MySQL username
define('DB_PASSWORD', '********');
  // ...and password (this isn't my real password)
```

```
define('DB_HOST', 'mysql.wordpressforall.com');
  // 99% chance you won't need to change this value
define('DB_CHARSET', 'utf8');
define('DB_COLLATE', '');


// Change each KEY to a different unique phrase.  You won't have
  to remember the phrases later,
// so make them long and complicated.  You can visit http://api.
  wordpress.org/secret-key/1.1/
// to get keys generated for you, or just make something up.
  Each key should have a different phrase.
define('AUTH_KEY', '!]/rQIt;T2eWAp.1hYVjs1GDuR+w(a[LM[~)xaS\"S4jY
  1-\\:o^48a%Y@CB5:}\"Q');
define('SECURE_AUTH_KEY', ' -~ b\'9!R`yc\'se2-xV`w
  CWD|>QAij0cu>.e xAV`C[\"D5o>E6l(\'h!zbq=&0NG');
define('LOGGED_IN_KEY', '~\\Difq+Wq@M&sWFC\\o6{l`#z3J=Du\")
  uHPW$>O5q Sw5,&JM5jlTT$ OQ}0LH}d=');


// You can have multiple installations in one database if you
  give each a unique prefix
$table_prefix  = 'wp_';   // Only numbers, letters, and under-
  scores please!


// Change this to localize WordPress.  A corresponding MO file
  for the
// chosen language must be installed to wp-content/languages.
// For example, install de.mo to wp-content/languages and set
  WPLANG to 'de'
// to enable German language support.
define ('WPLANG', '');


/* That's all, stop editing! Happy blogging. */


if ( !defined('ABSPATH') )
  define('ABSPATH', dirname(__FILE__) . '/');
require_once(ABSPATH . 'wp-settings.php');
?>
```

tip	When you're done setting up your wp-config file, make sure to save it as wp-config.php and not as wp-config-sample.php.

Choosing Your Blog's URL

Before you upload the files, you have one more thing to think about: your blog's URL structure.

Suppose that you've registered the domain www.wordpressforall.com, and you plan to host your WordPress blog there. You have a few options, including these:

- If you plan for your blog to be the primary content of your domain, you should upload the WordPress files directly to the site's root folder. That way, people who go directly to your URL will be greeted by your blog.

- If you plan to have a landing page or some other content living at the root of your site, you should upload the WordPress files to a subdirectory. To get to your blog, people will have to enter a URL like www.wordpressforall.com/blog. (In this example, you would create a subdirectory called blog at the root of the site and then upload all the WordPress files to that subdirectory.)

 If you want your blog's URL to be something other than www.*YOURBLOG*.com/wordpress, be sure to rename the default WordPress directory before you upload it to your site, or create the correctly named folder on your remote host and upload the WordPress files to that folder.

Installing WordPress

Now that you've figured out your blog's structure, you're ready to install
WordPress. You've spent a good amount of time working on your wp-config
file, so chances are that you won't run into any problems. Just use your
FTP client to upload your blog files to the directory you chose (refer to
"Choosing Your Blog's URL" earlier in this chapter). You should see a file
list something like **Figure 2.2**.

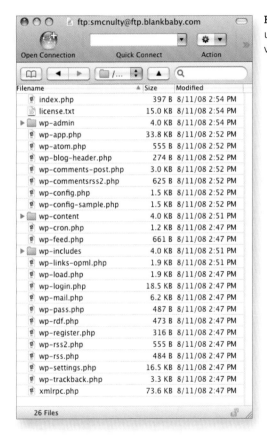

Figure 2.2 WordPress files
uploaded to a remote server
via the magic of CyberDuck.

After you've got all your files uploaded, the real fun begins.

Installing the software

To install the WordPress software, follow these steps:

1. Point your browser to the URL of your soon-to-be-functional blog.

   You'll be greeted by the WordPress installation screen (**Figure 2.3**).

Figure 2.3 The WordPress installation screen.

2. In the Blog Title text box, enter what you want your blog to be called.

   If you can't think of anything great at the moment, don't worry. You can easily change your blog's name later.

3. Enter your e-mail address in the Your E-Mail text box.

   Be sure to enter a valid address; WordPress uses it to send you the administrator account information it creates after installation.

4. Specify whether your blog should show up in search engines.

Not every blog is meant for public consumption. If you don't want people to find your blog easily, clear the check box titled Allow My Blog to Appear in Search Engines Like Google and Technorati. Otherwise, leave it checked. (How are you going to get famous if no one can Google you?)

5. Click the Install WordPress button.

After a couple of seconds, you should see a Success! screen containing details about the administrator account for your new blog (**Figure 2.4**).

6. Make a note of the password, which you'll need to log in to your blog for the first time.

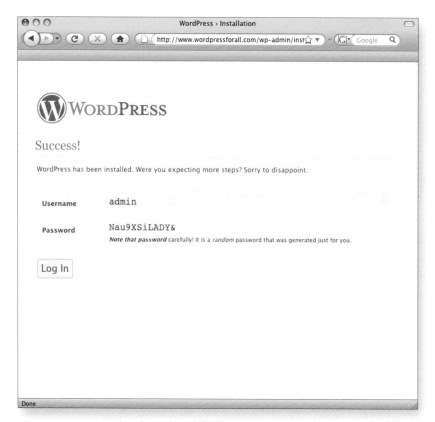

Figure 2.4 Success! The admin user and a random password have been created. (Don't try to use this password; I've changed it already.)

If, in your excitement, you clicked the Log In button before you jotted down the admin account information, worry not. WordPress also e-mailed that information to the address you provided in Step 3 (**Figure 2.5**).

New WordPress Blog
WordPress for All [wordpress@www.wordpressforall.com]

Sent: Monday, August 11, 2008 6:01 PM
To: McNulty, Scott

Your new WordPress blog has been successfully set up at:

http://www.wordpressforall.com

You can log in to the administrator account with the following information:

Username: admin
Password: Nau9XSiLADY&

We hope you enjoy your new blog. Thanks!

--The WordPress Team
http://wordpress.org/

Figure 2.5 WordPress thoughtfully e-mails the account information to you.

Logging in for the first time

The moment you've been waiting for is finally here. Click the Log In button, and you're whisked away to the WordPress login screen (**Figure 2.6**), which will become familiar to you in very short order.

Enter the admin account information and then click Log In. (Don't bother checking the Remember Me check box; in Chapter 3 I show you how to set up a different account that you'll use to log in to your blog in the future.)

Figure 2.6 The login screen.

Troubleshooting Common Installation Problems

As you see, installing WordPress isn't that tough, but sometimes bad things happen to good blogging software. A couple of common errors could happen when you're installing WordPress, and in this section, I show you how to work around them.

WordPress can't access database

Most problems occur when WordPress can't access your MySQL database. If you see an error message (**Figure 2.7**), make the following checks and then reload the install page:

Figure 2.7 A common installation error (but an easy one to correct).

- Double-check your DB_NAME, DB_USER, and DB_PASSWORD values. An easy way to make this check is to connect to your MySQL database using something other than WordPress. (Your Web hosting service should provide you a MySQL management tool.) If you can connect by using the values set in the wp-config file, reset the database user's password, and try again.

- Make sure that you're running the correct version of MySQL (version 4.0 or later).

PHP isn't enabled

The other common problem involves PHP and is also easy to fix. When you visit the URL to install WordPress, you may see a screenful of text starting with <?php instead of the install form. This text means that you don't have PHP enabled on your server.

Contact your Web hosting company or system administrator to find out how to enable PHP (and make sure that you're running PHP 4.3 or later). After you enable PHP, reload the install page. All should be well.

Managing User Accounts

The software is installed and running, and you've logged in to WordPress as an administrator. I bet that you think it's time to blog about something, right? Not so fast, Sparky. First things first: You need to change the password for the admin user (you'll never remember the randomly generated password that WordPress provided) and create a user account for yourself.

Why not just use the default admin user account that was created during the installation? Many people do, because it requires the least effort (we're all lazy people, when you come right down to it), but best practice is to use that admin account for administrative tasks only. That way, you don't have to do any tricks to get posts attributed to your name instead of the admin user name; all the user roles are clear from the get-go.

Managing User Profiles

The first time you log in to WordPress, you see the *Dashboard* (**Figure 3.1**), which I cover in more detail in Chapter 4. The Dashboard is the control center for your blog—the place where you access all sorts of options, statistics, and settings.

WordPress for All Visit Site

Write   Manage   Design   Comments   Settings   Plugins   Users

Figure 3.1 The WordPress Dashboard.

Resist the urge to click all over this feature with wild abandon, and focus your attention on the options in the top-right corner: Settings, Plugins, and Users. Your first order of business is to check out the default user profile, so click Users to open the Manage Users panel (**Figure 3.2**).

Figure 3.2 The Manage Users panel, listing the default admin user.

When you first open this panel, it lists only one user, called admin, but all the users of your blog will be listed here eventually. You'll use this panel to add new users (which I discuss later in this chapter) and to change the profiles of existing users (which I discuss next).

Changing a user profile

You can change a user's profile in either of two ways:

- **Editing yourself.** If you want to edit the account under which you're currently logged in, click the Your Profile link at the top of the page.

- **Editing someone else.** To edit another user's information, click that person's user name. (Not all users can do this, thanks to user roles. More on those in a bit.)

Either way, you end up on the Your Profile and Personal Options page, which has a bevy of options for you to set (**Figure 3.3**).

Figure 3.3 Your Profile and Personal Options page for the admin user.

Setting profile options

The profile options are grouped together, though I think the order of the options is a little odd. (I'd rather have the password options closer to the top of the page, for example. Something tells me that you're more likely to change your password than your user name.) In the following sections, I look at each group of options and explain what the options mean.

Visual Editor and Admin Color Scheme

You can set two visual aspects of the blog in your user profile: the Visual Editor and the Admin Color Scheme (**Figure 3.4**).

Figure 3.4 Setting the visual aspects of your blog.

Visual Editor. WordPress posts are written in HTML (Hypertext Markup Language), which is the tag-based language that Web pages are written in. Web browsers know how to interpret this code into the lovely words and images you read on people's blogs and Web sites. The only problem is that not everyone knows HTML; in fact, some people aren't interested in learning about HTML. They want to blog, not code. That's where the WordPress Visual Editor comes in.

The Visual Editor option turns the WordPress posting form (which I promise to talk more about in Chapter 6) into a WYSIWYG editor. A WYSIWYG (what you see is what you get) editor allows you to do things like insert links, format text, and create lists, using controls that are familiar to anyone who's ever edited a document in a word processor. Visual Editor generates all the HTML code for you, so that you can concentrate on writing that great post about your weekend.

note

Why even have an option to turn off Visual Editor? Before this feature was introduced in WordPress version 2, users had to hand-code their posts, and some people still like handcrafting their HTML (and argue that they can do it faster and better than any silly old WYSIWYG editor). If you agree with them, simply clear this check box.

Admin Color Scheme. You have two color-scheme choices for the WordPress admin interface. The Classic option will be familiar to anyone who's used previous versions of WordPress; the Fresh option is a relatively new color scheme that's a bit lighter. WordPress doesn't give you an easy way to create your own color schemes, which is a shame, but free add-ons to WordPress called *plug-ins* let you color to your heart's content. (I cover plug-ins in Chapter 13.)

note The color schemes, as well as everything else listed in the Your Profile and Personal Options page, are applied on a per-user basis. That means that I can choose to use the Classic color scheme, and another user of the same blog can pick Fresh. Everybody wins.

Name

Figure 3.5 shows the name settings for each user. WordPress is very flexible in the way it displays a user name; you just have to be sure to fill in as much information as possible to gain maximum flexibility. (WordPress can't display any information you haven't entered.)

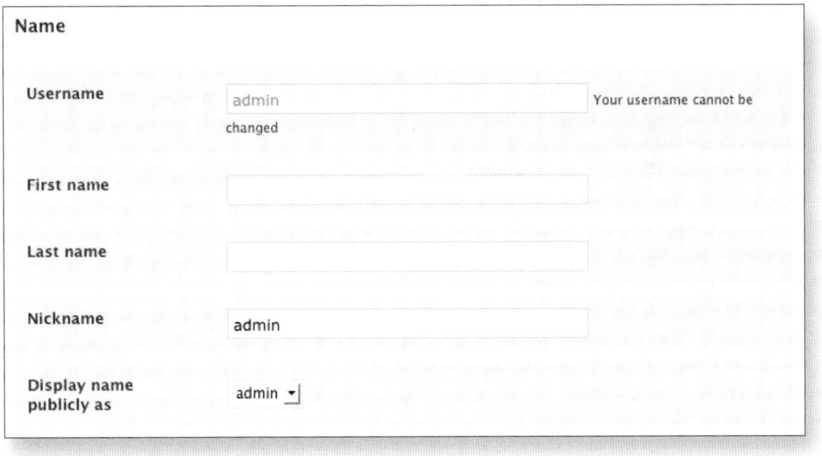

Name		
Username	admin	Your username cannot be
	changed	
First name		
Last name		
Nickname	admin	
Display name publicly as	admin ▾	

Figure 3.5 The Name options.

You can set these options:

- **Username.** You can't change this setting for the admin user. This user name is the one you'll use to log in to WordPress. Like your password, it's case sensitive.

- **First Name.** The user's first name goes in this text box (shocking, I know). This setting is optional, though filling in the text box gives you more name-display options, because WordPress won't be able to display your first name if it doesn't know what your first name is (and isn't it rude not to introduce yourself to your blog?).

- **Last Name.** The user's last name is also optional.

- **Nickname.** We're all familiar with the concept of nicknames. (In some circles, for example, I'm known as Dr. Awesome. Sure, those circles exist only in my imagination, but they still count.) The WordPress nickname option is just a name, other than user name or first name/last name, that you want to go by on your blog. You can have comments or posts credited to your nickname instead of your user name or real name.

- **Display Name Publicly As.** This setting is where that Nickname option pays off. You can choose to have your name displayed on posts and comments in a few ways: username, nickname, first name only, first name last, or last name first (**Figure 3.6**). Dr. Awesome is pleased.

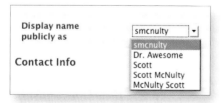

Figure 3.6 The available display names are based on the information provided in the Name section.

Contact Info

The Contact Info section (**Figure 3.7**) is straightforward, so I don't need to walk you through each option. Note, however, that an e-mail address is required so WordPress can send you notifications.

A variety of theme tweaks and plug-ins (see Chapter 12 and Chapter 13, respectively) can help you take advantage of contact information later—

perhaps by displaying instant-messaging user names on comments or user pages—so fill in as much or as little of this information as you're comfortable with.

Contact Info		
E-mail	wp@wordpressforall.com	Required
Website	http://	
AIM		
Yahoo IM		
Jabber / Google Talk		

Figure 3.7 An e-mail address is the only bit of contact info WordPress requires; the rest is just fun to have.

About Yourself

Figure 3.8 shows the "about" page for a user—you, in this case.

About Yourself	
Biographical Info	
	Share a little biographical information to fill out your profile. This may be shown publicly.
New Password	If you would like to change the password type a new one. Otherwise leave this blank.
	Type your new password again.
Password Strength	
Too short	Hint: Use upper and lower case characters, numbers and symbols like !"?$%^&(in your password.

Update Profile

Figure 3.8 WordPress wants to know about you, but the password section is the most important part.

Providing biographical info is optional, but as the Web becomes more of a social place, it's nice to share a little bit about yourself with your readers. (Besides, who doesn't like writing about himself or herself?) The New Password section, however, is required.

Changing your WordPress password is simple: Enter your new password twice (no need to enter your old password, because you can change your password only while you're already logged in), and click Update Profile. Clicking this button also saves the rest of the changes you made to your profile. If you want to change something in your profile but don't want to alter your password just leave both password boxes empty. The changes to your profile will be saved, and your password will remain the same.

Notice the Password Strength indicator below the password text boxes. This feature helps you pick a strong password but won't stop you from setting a weak password (it'll just be disappointed in you).

 tip   **The best passwords are long, complicated, and hard to guess. Don't use something common like *password* or your birthday. Do use a mix of letters (uppercase and lowercase), numbers, and symbols.**

Adding and Deleting Users

Now that the default admin user has a strong password, you're ready to create a user account for yourself. Are you excited? You're getting so close to blogging that I can almost taste it.

Adding a new user

To add a new user (in this case, yourself), follow these steps:

1. Click the Users link in the top-right corner of the Dashboard.

   The Manage Users panel opens (refer to Figure 3.2, earlier in this chapter).

2. In the Add New User section below the list of current users, enter the following required information:

- Username

- E-Mail

- Password

3. Choose a role from the Role drop-down menu.

I cover your choices in the next section, "Understanding user roles."

4. Click the Add User button.

You're all set.

Understanding user roles

WordPress has five user roles that you can assign to any user—one role per user. These roles define what a particular user can and can't do.

Here are the five roles, in decreasing order of power:

- Administrator

- Editor

- Author

- Contributor

- Subscriber

Each role sees, and can access, different things in WordPress's Dashboard.

In the following sections, I look at these roles and how they work in a typical blog.

Administrator

An Administrator has the power to do anything on the blog. This user can activate and deactivate plug-ins; modify themes; create and delete users; set global blog preferences; and delete, edit, and schedule all posts. The admin user that the WordPress installation creates has an Administrator user role, as should the first user account you create for yourself. If you're going to have other people blogging with you, chances are that they should have one of the other, less powerful roles.

Editor

The Editor role is one step below the Administrator role. Although a user with Administrator privileges has access to both sides of the blog—the technical side (such as themes, plug-ins, and users) and the content side (pages, posts, and comments)—a user with Editor privileges has full control of content only. An Editor can create posts, comments, links, and pages, as well as edit anything that another user creates. This person can even edit content that is created by an Administrator.

In a multiauthor blogging environment, give this role to someone who's in charge of all aspects of content, sort of like an editor-in-chief of a newspaper. This person can decide what gets published when.

Author

The Author role is even more focused on blog content than the Editor role. An Author can write and publish posts, as well as edit any comments on those posts. This person can't edit or approve comments on other people's work, however.

This role is suited for someone who (to continue the newspaper analogy) can serve as a staff writer. You trust this user to write well and publish only things that are worthy of your blog.

Contributor

I like to think of the people in Contributor roles as freelancers working on assignment. They can write posts and create pages, but they can't publish anything themselves. Everything a Contributor user writes is submitted for review. The post is marked as pending review until a user in an Editor or Administrator role approves and publishes it. Contributors can't approve comments on their own posts or edit their own posts.

Assign this role to people whom you're trying out on your blog. As you gain confidence in their abilities, you can promote them to Authors.

Subscriber

As the name suggests, a person in the Subscriber role isn't able to create posts, edit users, or do any sort of administration of the blog. You can set your blog so that only registered Subscribers can post comments; I explain how in the next section, "Registering users." You also can allow people to register themselves as users, generally in the Subscriber role; again, see the next section for details.

Subscribers can log in to the WordPress admin area, but they can only change their user information: set a new password or change a bio.

Registering users

You don't have to add every user to your blog manually. This process could get quite cumbersome if you require people to register with your site before they can leave comments. (If you get more than a few readers, you won't want to have to create their user accounts by hand.) Luckily, WordPress provides a way for people to register themselves. This feature is turned off by default, but you can enable it very simply.

In the Add New User section of the Manage Users panel, you see a line that says *Users cannot currently register themselves, but you can manually create users here.* Clicking the words *register themselves* takes you to the General Settings page of your blog (which I cover fully in Chapter 5). **Figure 3.9** shows the membership options.

Membership	☐ Anyone can register
	☐ Users must be registered and logged in to comment
New User Default Role	Subscriber ▾

Figure 3.9 Membership options.

The Membership section has two check-box options:

- **Anyone Can Register:** Check this box to allow any visitor to your site to register as a user.

- **Users Must Be Registered and Logged in to Comment:** Enable this check box to require commenters to be registered—a way to discourage comment spam (see the sidebar in this section).

You can also set the role for any user account registered in this fashion by making a choice from the New User Default Role drop-down menu (**Figure 3.10**). The default setting is Subscriber.

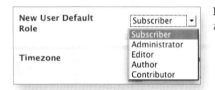

Figure 3.10 Assigning a role to a new user.

tip	I suggest that you keep this menu set to Subscriber. You don't want random people to create their own posts on your blog, and you certainly don't want just anyone to administer your blog.

Comments on Comment Spam

The WordPress user-registration feature was designed to combat *comment spam*—comments on your blog that have no relevance to your blog, posted only to add links to other sites. Most of the time, actual people aren't leaving these comments; rather, software programs called *bots* trawl the Internet for blogs. When bots find a blog, they start hammering it with spurious comments, thereby creating comment spam.

Because WordPress uses a well-known URL structure for the new user form (which is the same across all WordPress installations), someone could craft a bot that signs up for several fake accounts on your blog. These accounts could then be used to leave comment spam, though more often than not, the accounts are simply created and nothing more is done.

In Chapter 13, I show you how to combat comment spam by using some great plug-ins.

Changing user roles

During the course of your blog's life you may want to promote someone from a Contributor to an Editor, or make an Author into a Contributor just for fun. (Isn't holding power over something a joy?) All you have to do is follow these steps:

1. Click the Users link in the Dashboard to open the Manage Users panel.

2. In the list of your blog's users, check the box next to the user whose role you want to change.

3. From the Change Role To drop-down menu above the list of users (**Figure 3.11**), choose the new role you want to assign.

4. Click the Change button.

   That's it. Now the user now has more (or less) power.

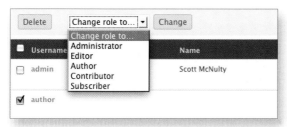

Figure 3.11 Pick a new role from the menu.

 Only Administrator users can change user roles.

Deleting users

Deleting a user is much like changing a user's role. Follow these steps:

1. Click the Users link in the Dashboard to open the Manage Users panel.

2. In the list of your blog's users, check the box next to the user you want to delete.

3. Click the Delete button.

The Delete Users panel opens (**Figure 3.12**). Because WordPress assumes that all that users are making content for your blog, you have to tell it what you want it to do with this user's content (if any).

Figure 3.12
The Delete Users panel.

4. Choose an option to specify what to do with the user's content.

You have two choices:

- **Delete All Posts and Links.** Selecting this radio button makes it as though the user you're deleting never existed. All of his posts and links will be deleted from your site.

- **Attribute All Posts and Links to X,** where X is another user. This option is the more interesting, and more clever, of the two choices. The user account will still be deleted, which means that user won't be able to log in and add more content, but the existing content won't be deleted. Instead, the deleted user's posts and links will be displayed under the user name of the person you choose from this drop-down menu.

note Even if you delete all of a user's posts, comments on those posts will remain on display. If you want to get rid of all traces of that user on your blog, you'll have to delete the comments on her posts manually. Keep in mind, though, that deleting comments generally is considered to be bad form unless the comments are abusive in some way. Use your power wisely.

4

The Dashboard

The Dashboard (**Figure 4.1**) is the first thing you see when you log into any installation of WordPress. It's your captain's chair, the tower from which you overlook the grandeur of your digital kingdom, the window into your blog, and a dozen more clichés.

The Dashboard provides information at a glance about a variety of WordPress-related items through six panels:

- Right Now
- Recent Comments
- Incoming Links
- WordPress Development Blog
- Plugins
- Other WordPress News

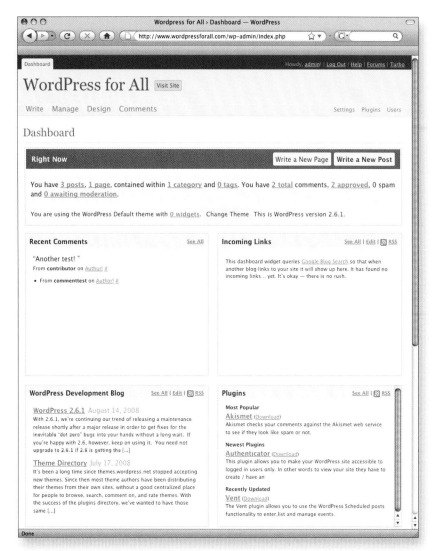

Figure 4.1 The WordPress Dashboard, in all its glory.

Out of the box, the Dashboard customization options are limited, but they can be expanded with—you guessed it—plug-ins. This isn't to say that you don't have any options out of the gate, though. As long as you're logged in as a user in the Administrator role, you can change a few things.

In this chapter, you take a look at the anatomy of the Dashboard. Along the way, I point out what you can change.

Right Here: Right Now

At the top of the Dashboard, you see the Right Now panel (**Figure 4.2**), which has an orange header—no doubt to catch your attention. Because WordPress is all about creating content, the panel has two big buttons: Write a New Page and Write a New Post. Clicking either of those buttons takes you directly to the posting form so you can get down to the good stuff (which I promise to talk about very shortly, in Chapter 6).

Figure 4.2 Right Now gives you easy access to the most important aspect of your blog: the content.

Below that orange banner, you see some statistics about your blog, complete with hyperlinks. A fresh installation of WordPress comes with one post and a comment to give you a good starting place. Clicking one of the statistics links takes you to the related section of WordPress, as follows:

- The post link takes you to the Manage Posts panel, where you can edit or create posts (depending on your role).

- The page link takes you to the Manage Pages panel.

- The category link shows you how many categories you currently have in your blog. Click this link to add, edit, or delete categories.

- The comments page is broken up into four subsections: total comments, number of approved comments, number of spam comments, and number of comments awaiting moderation. When the number in any of those categories is greater than zero, you can click the link to perform comment-specific actions.

Below all that information about the content of your blog, you get some info about the blog itself: the current theme, which determines what your blog looks like, and the number of widgets the theme is using. (See Chapter 11 for details on themes and widgets.) Clicking the widgets link takes you to the Widgets panel, which allows you to add or remove widgets. You can change your current theme by clicking the Change Theme button.

Finally, the Right Now panel displays the version of WordPress you're running. If a new version is available, a note here alerts you to update your software (**Figure 4.3**).

WordPress 2.6.1 is available! Please update now.

Figure 4.3 When a WordPress update is available, this alert pops up on the Dashboard.

Meeting the Public: Comments and Links

The next two panels, right below Right Now, concern the lifeblood of any blog: comments and external links. You'll never forget the first time someone comments on one of your blog posts, and you'll be thrilled when you find the first Web site *not* run by you that's linking to your blog.

Recent Comments panel

As you might expect, the Recent Comments panel (**Figure 4.4**) displays recent comments that folks have left on your blog. It also alerts you to any comments that are awaiting moderation. The pound sign (#) is a link directly to that comment. You can also click the See All link in the top-right corner to manage all the comments on your blog.

Figure 4.4
Recent Comments are displayed in this panel.

Incoming Links panel

The Incoming Links panel (**Figure 4.5**) is a great way to see what other people are saying about your blog on their blogs. This feature uses Google Blog Search to see what blogs are linking to yours and reports back to you. When you first install WordPress, there won't be any links to your blog, so your panel will look like Figure 4.5. As you start to blog, though, you'll start to build your audience, and people will start linking to you. It won't happen overnight, but with some work, it'll happen sooner than you think.

Figure 4.5 Incoming Links tells you how many people are (or aren't) linking to your blog.

Clicking the See All link opens a new browser window or tab to a Google Blog Search for your blog's URL. This way, you see all the blogs linking back to your blog—not just those in the panel.

You can customize this panel to a degree by clicking the Edit link. When you do, the panel expands as you see in **Figure 4.6**.

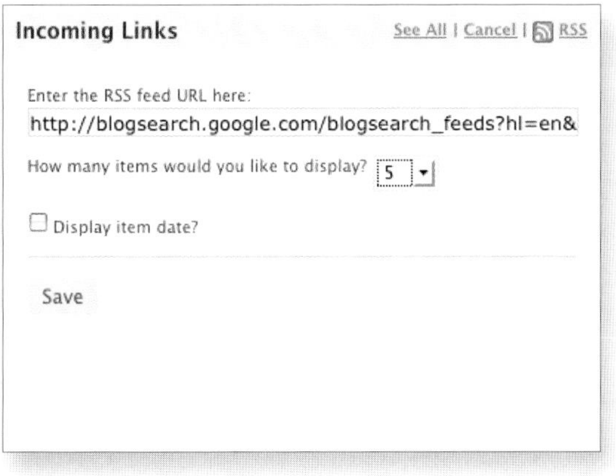

Incoming Links   See All | Cancel | 🔊 RSS

Enter the RSS feed URL here:
http://blogsearch.google.com/blogsearch_feeds?hl=en&

How many items would you like to display? [5 ▾]

☐ Display item date?

Save

Figure 4.6 You can plug in the RSS feed of your favorite blog search engine here and make the Incoming Links panel display what you want to see.

You can set the following options in the expanded Incoming Links panel:

- **RSS feed:** By default, this panel uses Google Blog Search. But if you prefer to use another search engine that provides an RSS feed of results, you can enter the URL of its RSS feed here. (I discuss RSS feeds in more detail in Chapter 5.)

- **Number of items to display:** Choose the number you want from the drop-down menu. You can display 1 item to 20 items.

- **Display date:** If you check this check box, the date of the link appears alongside the link itself.

- **Subscribe to feed:** The RSS link and orange RSS icon in the top-right corner of the panel allow you to subscribe to this panel's results in your favorite newsreader. That way, you'll know the moment anyone links to one of your brilliant posts (which will happen often; I can tell just by the way you read).

Whatever you do in this panel, click Save when you're done to tell WordPress to accept your changes.

 You can't customize this panel too much, and the same goes for the rest of the panels featured in this chapter. Neither can you rearrange the order that they're displayed in or hide them from view. This functionality isn't enabled by default. In Chapter 13, however, I discuss a plug-in that allows you to do much more with the Dashboard.

Getting Technical: Development Blog and Plugins

The next two panels of the Dashboard are WordPress Development Blog and Plugins. Both panels display RSS feeds: one for the Development blog, and the other for a list of the most popular, newest, and most recently updated plug-ins (**Figure 4.7**). You can subscribe in each panel to the RSS feed, and you can click See All in each panel to view the Web sites that the feeds come from.

Figure 4.7 These two panels are your windows on the greater WordPress community.

The Development Blog panel has an Edit link, which means you can customize it somewhat. When you click that link, you see an expanded panel (**Figure 4.8**) with options slightly different from those in the expanded Incoming Links panel.

Figure 4.8 The expanded WordPress Development Blog panel.

In addition to RSS feed, number of items to display, and item date, you can set these options in the expanded panel:

- **Feed title:** The default is WordPress Development Blog, but you can change the title to anything you want, and the panel's name then changes in the interface. You could use this setting in combination with the RSS feed setting to display a different blog's content in this panel and have it labeled as such. Neato.

- **Display of item content:** Because this panel is a mini-RSS reader, it only makes sense that you can display the content of entries.

Only excerpts are shown in this panel's limited space; disable this option if you want to see just titles.

- **Display of item author:** In keeping with the mini-RSS reader idea, you can also display the author of the entry if it is available in the feed.

The Development Blog panel is also known as the Primary Feed panel because you can display whatever RSS feed you want in it.

The Plugin panel, on the other hand, offers no customization options. You can subscribe to the Plugin RSS feed, however, so you can stay on top of things.

Keeping Current: Other WordPress News

The final panel of the Dashboard, Other WordPress News (**Figure 4.9**), showcases blogs of that are either written by WordPress developers or devoted to WordPress.

Other WordPress News				See All	Edit	🔊 RSS
Be Kind, Educate	WordCamp San Francisco 2008 Photos	WordCamp 2008 San Francisco - Great Fun.	WordPress Theme Releases for 08/17	Secure Coding with WordPress - WordCamp SF
Weblog Tools Collection	*Matt*	*Lorelle on WP*	*Weblog Tools Collection*	*Mark Jaquith*
WordCamp SF Coverage	WordPress Plugin Releases for 08/16	What Does the Blurb on Top of Plugins Link Mean?	WordCamp Utah	WP Plugin: "Where did they go from here" Updated
Matt	*Weblog Tools Collection*	*Weblog Tools Collection*	*Alex King*	*Weblog Tools Collection*
Maintenance Update: WordPress 2.6.1 Released	WordPress 2.6.1	WordPress 2.6.1	Are you going to WordCamp San Francisco?	WordPress 57%
Weblog Tools Collection	*Ryan Boren*	*Dev Blog*	*Weblog Tools Collection*	*Matt*

Figure 4.9 The Other WordPress News panel.

This panel is also known as the Secondary Feed panel.

When you click the Edit link in this panel, you see yet another slightly different set of options in a Secondary Feed panel (**Figure 4.10**). You can set the feed URL, give the panel a title, and choose how many items to display. No matter what feed you choose, the panel displays news items in boxes, as you see in Figure 4.9.

Figure 4.10
The Secondary Feed panel allows you to display any RSS feed you want.

Beyond the Dashboard

The top of every WordPress admin page features a few links of interest. The first link, on the far-left side, is labeled Dashboard (**Figure 4.11**). This link takes you back to the Dashboard no matter where you find yourself in the WordPress interface.

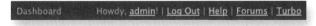

Figure 4.11 The Dashboard link on a WordPress admin page.

The right side of the page contains a mix of links to internal and external resources:

- **User name.** The first link is your user name, which takes you to your profile page (see Chapter 3).

- **Log Out.** The Log Out link logs you out of the WordPress administrative interface.

- **Help.** This link, like Forum (see the next bullet point), takes you to an external Web site that contains information about WordPress. Help points to the WordPress Codex (http://codex.wordpress.org/), which contains more information about WordPress than you'll ever want to read.

- **Forum.** The Forum link takes you to the WordPress Forums page (http://wordpress.org/support/), where you can post questions, read other people's experiences with WordPress, and find out some tips and tricks.

- **Turbo.** The final link, Turbo, is the most interesting. Click it to launch a pop-up window (**Figure 4.12**) that describes WordPress support for the Gears feature. Turbo makes your WordPress Dashboard faster by using Gears to store some of the Dashboard files locally, on your own computer. Your browser doesn't need to retrieve the files from the remote server, which saves some time.

Figure 4.12 Enabling Turbo for your WordPress installation.

 note Gears supports only certain browsers in certain operating systems, so be sure to check out http://gears.google.com/ for more information.

5

Futureproofing Your Blog

There's one last bit of business to take care of before I delve into populating your blog with some awesome content: your blog's settings. This chapter is titled "Futureproofing Your Blog" because the decisions you make now will affect how you and your readers interact with your blog.

Clicking the Settings link in the top navigation bar, which appears on all pages in the WordPress administrative interface (**Figure 5.1** on the next page), takes you, surprisingly enough, to your blog's Settings tab. (You start in the General Settings section.) In addition to setting general options, this page is where you specify how you write posts, how those posts are displayed, and who can read what.

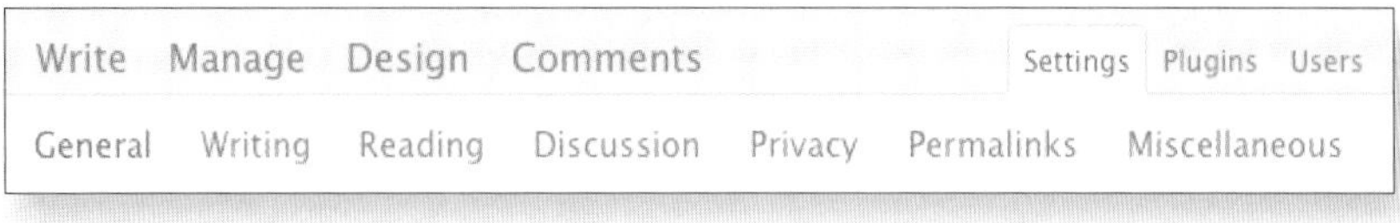

| Write | Manage | Design | Comments | | | Settings | Plugins | Users |
| General | Writing | Reading | Discussion | Privacy | Permalinks | Miscellaneous | | |

Figure 5.1 The WordPress settings navigation bar. All your settings dreams await you.

General Settings

When you first click the Settings link, you see the general settings for your blog. Many of these settings are defined in the wp-config.php file (refer to Chapter 2), but you can change them at any time (**Figure 5.2**).

After you change any of the settings listed in this chapter, make sure to click the Save Changes button at the bottom of the page. If you don't, your changes won't be saved, and you'll need to make them again.

Blog name and tagline

The Blog Title and Tagline options (**Figure 5.3**) are often used in a blog's header, so make sure that you like the name you give your blog.

Something to keep in mind: Should your blog succeed, there's a chance that you'll be known by your blog's name. In some circles I am known as Blankbaby, which a weaker man might not be able to handle. Name your blog well.

Figure 5.2
Your blog's General
Settings page.

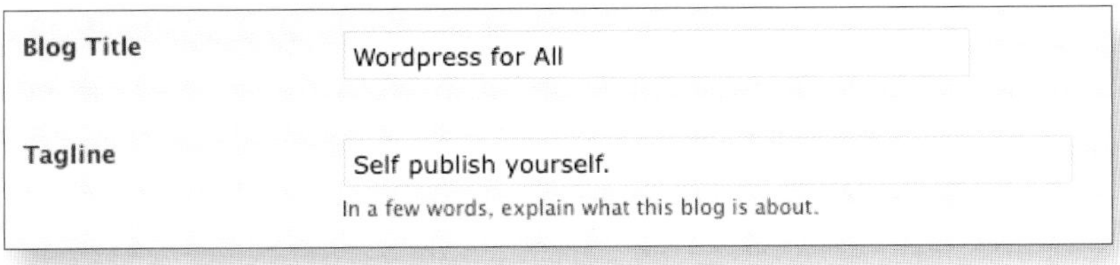

Figure 5.3 Your blog's title and tagline are often the things people remember most.

WordPress and blog URLs

The WordPress Address (URL) and Blog Address (URL) options (**Figure 5.4**) aren't the same, though it certainly seems that they would be. The WordPress URL points to the directory on the Web server that houses your installation of WordPress, whereas the blog URL is the address people enter to get to your blog. In most cases these URLs are the same, but you can separate the files that make up the WordPress application itself from the contents of your blog, as I discuss later in this chapter.

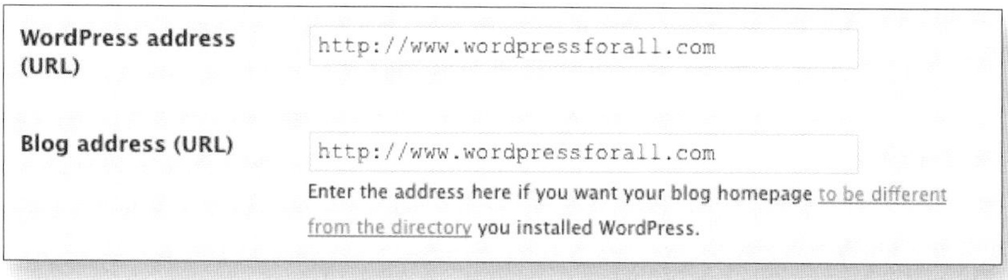

WordPress address (URL)	http://www.wordpressforall.com
Blog address (URL)	http://www.wordpressforall.com
	Enter the address here if you want your blog homepage to be different from the directory you installed WordPress.

Figure 5.4 WordPress Address points to where WordPress itself is installed; Blog Address is the URL of your blog.

Storing WordPress and content files together

WordPress, as you know, is made up of various folders and files. By default, those files are stored in the same directory, as you see in **Figure 5.5**. But if your blog is just one component of a multifaceted Web site, you may want to have tighter control of your directory structure.

Confused? Consider a concrete example: the WordPress for All blog. I uploaded the contents of the wordpress folder, which I got from WordPress.org, to my Web site's root directory. As you see in Figure 5.5, that folder is now chockablock with all the files and directories that WordPress needs.

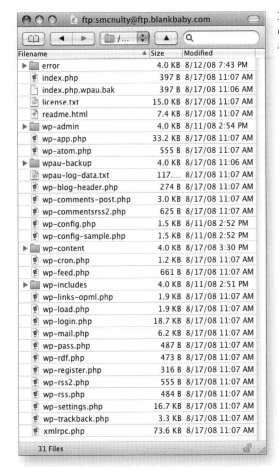

Figure 5.5 A directory that contains both WordPress and blog files.

Separating WordPress and content files

Moving all those WordPress files into their own directory would really neaten things. This change won't have any noticeable ramifications for your readers but will affect the people who create content for your blog, no matter what roles they play. (Flip back to Chapter 3 for details on user roles.)

Again, consider the example WordPress for All blog. As it's set up at the moment, people log into the administrative side by going to www.*yourblogname*.com/wp-admin. Moving the WordPress files to their own directory would change the URL for logging in to the admin interface.

Separating WordPress and content files is easy. Just follow these steps:

1. Create a new directory to hold the WordPress files.

   For this exercise, create a directory called wordpress.

   Next, because you're moving the entire WordPress application, you need to make sure that WordPress knows where all its files are before you move them.

2. On the General Settings page, change the WordPress Address (URL) option to reflect the future home of your WordPress installation.

3. Click Save Changes.

   You'll get an error message. Don't worry about it.

4. Move all your WordPress files to your new wordpress directory, but leave the index.php file in the root directory (**Figure 5.6**).

The index.php file makes the blog URL work.

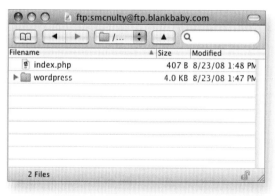

Figure 5.6 WordPress installed in the wordpress directory. Much neater.

The index.php file needs one edit; then you'll be all done.

5. Open the index.php file in your favorite text editor and look for the following section:

```
require('./wp-blog-header.php');
```

This bit of code tells the index file where your WordPress files live, and because you just moved them, the code is pointing to the wrong place. (By default, this file assumes that all the WordPress files are in the same directory where it resides.)

6. Add the name of the new directory to the code in Step 5, using this format:

```
require('./directory/wp-blog-header.php');
```

For this exercise, you moved the files to a directory called wordpress, so change the code to this:

```
require('./wordpress/wp-blog-header.php');
```

7. Save the file.

Everything works exactly as it did before, but your files are better organized, as a glance at the General Settings page shows (**Figure 5.7**).

Figure 5.7 New URL settings.

E-mail address

The important thing to remember for the E-Mail Address setting (**Figure 5.8**) is to supply WordPress a valid e-mail address. WordPress will send notifications about your blog in general to the address you enter, and you'll want to get them.

E-mail address	admin@wordpressforall.com
	This address is used for admin purposes, like new user notification.

Figure 5.8 All e-mail notifications will be sent to the address you enter here.

Membership options

I cover these options in Chapter 3, so I'll keep this discussion brief.

In the Membership section (**Figure 5.9**), checking the Anyone Can Register check box allows visitors to your blog to create user accounts. If you select the other option, limiting comments to registered users, you have more control of your blog. You can also set what role is automatically assigned to new users, with the default being the least powerful role, Subscriber.

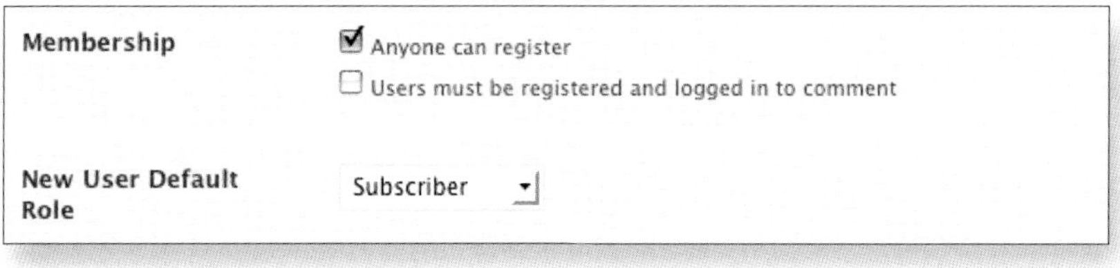

Figure 5.9 Do you want people to register their own accounts on your blog? Make sure that you give them a proper default role.

Time options

Time is our most precious resource, and it isn't renewable. Luckily, WordPress gives you a lot of control over how time is displayed and kept in your WordPress blog. You can set the time zone, date and time formats, and the day on which your week starts.

Time zone

Setting your time zone (**Figure 5.10**) is straightforward, but support for daylight saving time (DST) isn't built in. You have to change the time manually when DST comes around (assuming that you live somewhere that participates in DST).

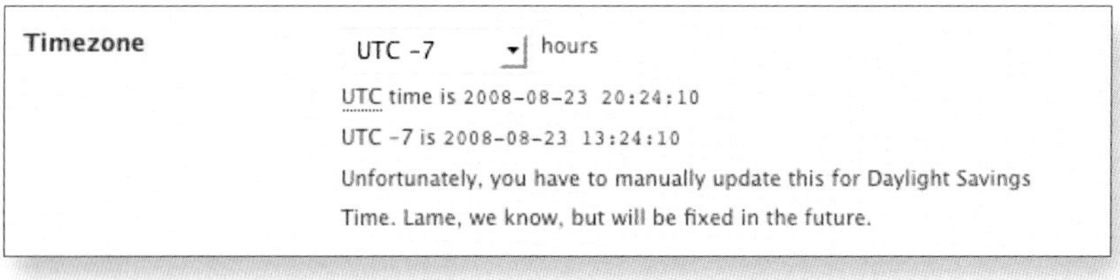

Figure 5.10 The WordPress Timezone setting doesn't automatically account for daylight saving time.

note WordPress employs Coordinated Universal Time (UTC), which is known casually as Greenwich Mean Time. Technically, UTC and GMT have some slight differences, but for purposes of this discussion, they're the same.

Date and time formats

The Date Format and Time Format settings (**Figure 5.11**) are a little more interesting. WordPress time-stamps all the content in your blog for a variety of reasons, and this section allows you to specify how the time is displayed. The time function of WordPress is written in PHP, as is the rest of WordPress, which means that your customization options are pretty wide open.

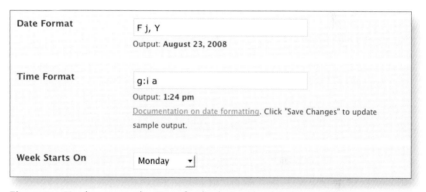

Figure 5.11 You have several options for displaying the date in your blog.

 tip If you want more information about the various date parameters that WordPress accepts, check out the PHP date-function documentation at http://us3.php.net/date.

 note You need to save your changes before you see a preview of the new time format.

Table 5.1 lists some of the most common date formats.

Code	Resulting Date
F j, Y	August 23, 2008
F-m-d	2008-08-23
d.m.F	23.08.2008
g:i a	7:03 p.m.
g:i a e	7:03 p.m. UTC
g:i a T	8:10 pm GMT
H:i:s	20:12:07

Table 5.1 WordPress Date Formats

Start of week

Finally, this section of the General Settings page allows to you tell WordPress which day of the week to treat as the start of the week. The default setting is Monday, but you can choose any day of the week from the Week Starts On drop down-menu (refer to Figure 5.11).

Writing Settings

The settings I discuss in this section define how you post on your blog. From enabling the ability to post via e-mail to determining the size of the box in which you type your posts, the Writing Settings panel is the place to set your writing options.

Posting from WordPress

The posting settings, shown in **Figure 5.12**, affect the experience of posting on your blog from within the WordPress application itself.

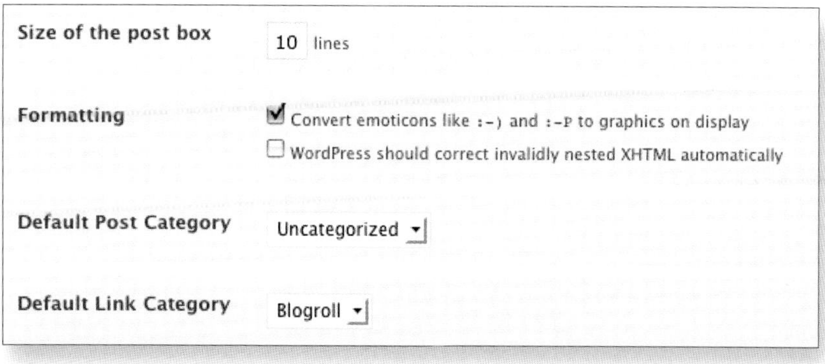

Size of the post box	10 lines
Formatting	☑ Convert emoticons like :-) and :-P to graphics on display ☐ WordPress should correct invalidly nested XHTML automatically
Default Post Category	Uncategorized ▾
Default Link Category	Blogroll ▾

Figure 5.12 Posting options abound in the Writing Settings panel.

Post-box size

By default, the post box is 10 lines long by default, which I find to be more than big enough for my purposes. If you need more space to write, feel free to change the Size of Post Box value. The maximum is 100 lines, though I can't imagine why you would want your posting box to be that large.

Formatting: Emoticons

Emoticons (also known as *smileys*) are all the rage with the kids these days, or so I'm told, and WordPress can cater to the emoticon set. If you check the pertinent check box in the Formatting section, WordPress automatically converts emoticons to graphic representations of the various smiley faces (**Figure 5.13**). This functionality can also be triggered by typing certain key terms, such as **:lol:** and **:cool:**.

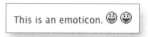
This is an emoticon.

Figure 5.13 Emoticons make me smile.

Enabling emoticons allows both commenters and bloggers to use them.

tip For a full list of the default emoticons and the text needed to insert them, check out the official Smilies WordPress Codex page at http://codex.wordpress.org/Using_Smilies. ;)

You can add your own custom smilies by replacing the files in *root/* wp-includes/images/smilies, where *root* is the directory in which WordPress is installed. Be sure to replace the files with small GIF files that are named the same way.

Formatting: XHTML

The second check box in the Formatting section—WordPress Should Correct Invalidly Nested XHTML Automatically—is decidedly less whimsical. XHTML is a stricter form of HTML, which you are no doubt familiar with. Both XHTML and HTML are tag-based languages. XHTML, however, requires every tag to have a closing tag, whereas HTML is a little more lax in that department. If you want your blog's code to validate, you should check this check box; otherwise, you can safely ignore it. (That sound you just heard was Web geeks everywhere passing out after reading this advice.)

Default post and link categories

You can set default categories for both posts and links. Choose a category from the Default Post Category or Default Link Category drop-down menu, and any new post or link automatically falls into that category. (You can add more categories or remove the defaults on individual posts and links when you edit them. See Chapter 6 for information about settings for posts and Chapter 9 for details on links.).

Links and posts don't share category lists, so you'll see a different list of values in each drop-down menu. (By default, the only post category you see is Uncategorized, and the only link category is Blogroll.) It would be nice if you could have WordPress *not* apply a category to new posts and links. I don't know about you, but I blog about a wide range of topics, and no single category applies to all my posts and links. Perhaps a future version of WordPress will allow me—and bloggers like me—to turn off default categorization.

Remote posting

You have two choices for posting on your blog:

- Use the posting tools in the WordPress administration interface.

- Use a third-party desktop/mobile application to post to your blog.

The second option is known as *remote posting* in WordPress speak.

The protocols required to use a third-party blogging application (see the nearby sidebar) are disabled by default in WordPress as of version 2.6. Because most people use WordPress to post, the developers decided to close off all unnecessary protocols and possible attack vectors.

That being said, I'm unaware of any security holes in either remote posting protocols, so one of the first things I do in a WordPress 2.6 installation is enable both Atom Publishing Protocol and XML-RPC in the Remote Publishing section (**Figure 5.14**).

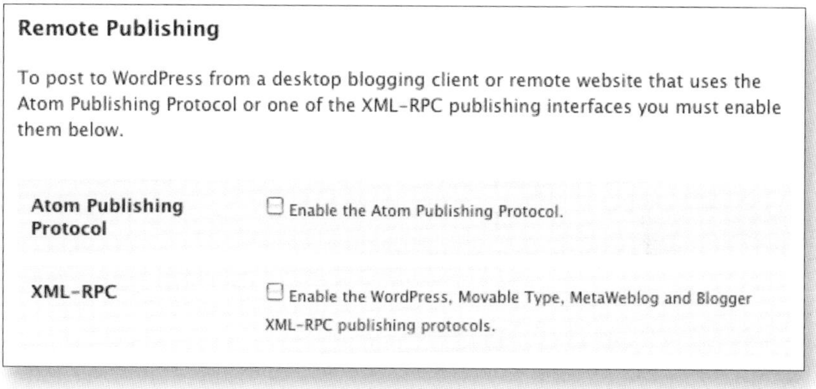

Remote Publishing

To post to WordPress from a desktop blogging client or remote website that uses the Atom Publishing Protocol or one of the XML–RPC publishing interfaces you must enable them below.

Atom Publishing Protocol   ☐ Enable the Atom Publishing Protocol.

XML–RPC   ☐ Enable the WordPress, Movable Type, MetaWeblog and Blogger XML–RPC publishing protocols.

Figure 5.14 There are two kinds of bloggers: those who use a third-party blogging application and those who post directly in the WordPress interface.

If you don't plan to use a third-party blogging tool, you should leave these protocols disabled.

Third-Party vs. WordPress Posting Tools

Why would you use third-party applications to post to your WordPress blog? They have several advantages over the WordPress posting form:

- Because they're full-fledged applications, they have access to features in your operating system (spell checking being a big one).

- They allow you to write and store drafts locally, in case you want to mull over your subject for a while.

- You can use one application to post across multiple blogs.

Here are a few blogging clients to check out:

- **BlogJet (Windows).** Lots of bloggers swear by this tool. It's a little pricey (about $40 at this writing), but it has a well-thought-out interface and a slew of features, including single-post publication to multiple blogs, drafts, and automatic insertion of the title of whatever you're listening to in iTunes or Windows Media Player. Find it at www.codingrobots.com/blogjet.

- **Windows Live Writer (Windows).** This application is a free blog editor from Microsoft. If you're familiar with Microsoft Office, Live Writer will feel like home to you. For details, check http://get.live.com/writer/overview.

- **ecto (Mac OS X).** This blogging client offers a ton of features, including creating Amazon.com affiliate links and searching. ecto costs $17.95 and is available at http://infinite-sushi.com/software/ecto.

- **MarsEdit (Mac OS X).** My blog editor of choice, MarsEdit doesn't have as many bells and whistles as ecto, but I like its streamlined interface more. MarsEdit costs $29.95. Get it at www.red-sweater.com/marsedit.

Posting via e-mail

Wouldn't it be great if you could e-mail your blog and have it post the contents of that e-mail? WordPress gives you that capability, though this feature is pretty rudimentary at this point. You have to provide WordPress login credentials for a POP email account. The account must be accessible via POP because WordPress actually logs in to this account and checks for messages.

The idea is pretty simple: You set up a secret e-mail address that WordPress can check (the General Settings page provides three suggestions; **Figure 5.15**) provide login information to WordPress, and then send an e-mail to the secret address. WordPress checks the e-mail account and posts the contents of the e-mail to your blog, using the subject as the title of the post and the body of the message as the body of the post.

Post via e-mail

To post to WordPress by e-mail you must set up a secret e-mail account with POP3 access. Any mail received at this address will be posted, so it's a good idea to keep this address very secret. Here are three random strings you could use: UCZ1H1Oi, JRXAUApK, kWEHYKoX.

Figure 5.15 WordPress suggests secret addresses.

Sadly, WordPress can't check this account for e-mail on its own. You have to visit a URL that fires off a process that checks the account and posts the e-mailed post. (That URL is www.*yourblogname*.com/*wordpress*/wp-mail.php, where *wordpress* is the directory where you've installed WordPress.) The situation isn't ideal, but you can use a couple of work-arounds:

- To the footer of your blog, add a frame that includes some code that visits the address where the wp-mail.php file is located. Every time one of your blog pages is loaded, WordPress checks the e-mail account for e-mailed posts.

- Use cron, a Unix program that runs tasks on a schedule, to visit wp-mail.php at regular intervals. Check your Web host's documentation to see whether you have access to cron on the host's servers.

note I should point out that posting via e-mail doesn't support posting attachments, which means that you can't e-mail a picture to your WordPress blog and have it post automatically. You can add this functionality with a plug-in, however; I discuss that feature in Chapter 13.

You need to provide WordPress the following information before you can post via e-mail (**Figure 5.16**):

Mail Server	mail.example.com
	Port 110
Login Name	login@example.com
Password	password
Default Mail Category	Uncategorized ▾

Figure 5.16 Settings for the post via e-mail feature.

- **Mail Server.** This section actually has two parts: the Mail Server field and the Port field. As you see in Figure 5.16, you need to provide the address of your mail server so that WordPress knows where to check for the e-mailed posts. The port number is set to the default for POP3 (110), which is the only kind of e-mail account WordPress can check. If your e-mail server uses a different port, make sure to set it here. (Ask your postmaster for this information if you don't have it.)

- **Login Name.** In this text box, enter the name of the account that WordPress will use to log in to the account. Typically, this account is the same as the e-mail address used for the e-mail posting.

- **Password.** This setting is the password of the e-mail account you set up for mobile blogging.

 note   WordPress doesn't obscure what you type in this text box, so don't enter a password where prying eyes may be lurking.

- **Default Mail Category.** Much as you set a default category for every post and link in WordPress, you can set a default category for posts sent via e-mail. You may think that having a default category for regular posts and links is silly, but this option makes perfect sense. Adding a category like Posts from On the Go or Moblogging tells your readers that you tapped the post out on a tiny keyboard, so it may contain a few more typos than usual.

note Although I think this WordPress feature isn't ready for prime time, it's worth noting that blogs hosted on WordPress.com don't get this functionality at all.

Update services

You started a blog because you want people to read what you post, right? One way to get readers, in the crowded blogosphere, is to ping an update service—a central place that keeps a list of recently updated blogs. When you post a new entry to your blog, you ping (or tell) the update service that you posted something, and the service duly notes it. When someone asks that service for recently updated posts, it returns a link to your new post, along with other recently posted entries.

You can find lots of update services out there, which has led Automattic (the company that runs WordPress.com, made up of many of the people behind WordPress itself) to create Ping-o-Matic. Ping-o-Matic is a central update service that updates the other update services (whoa—meta!). WordPress ships configured to tell Ping-o-Matic whenever you post something, and the service then informs a host of other update services.

You can remove Ping-o-Matic simply by deleting that entry in the Update Services section (**Figure 5.17**), or you can add another update service by pasting the proper URL into the text box. (The update service you're adding should have documentation that includes the proper URL to enter.) Be sure to separate URLs with line breaks by pressing Enter or Return after each URL.

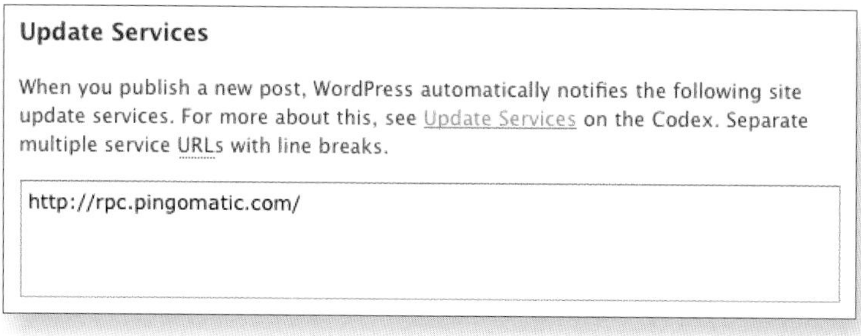

Update Services

When you publish a new post, WordPress automatically notifies the following site update services. For more about this, see Update Services on the Codex. Separate multiple service URLs with line breaks.

http://rpc.pingomatic.com/

Figure 5.17 The update service you list here tells people when your blog has been updated.

Reading Settings

The other side of the blogging coin is reading. Your blog won't be much fun if no one reads it, though don't be fooled into thinking that your blog isn't a success if you reach a small number of people. A small blog that you use to keep in touch with friends and relatives is just as important as a large political or tech blog with millions of readers. (Personally, I find small personal blogs to be much more interesting than large professional blogs, and I write for one of those large blogs!).

You do have a few decisions to make about how your blog content is consumed, no matter how many readers you end up with.

Setting the front page

Some people refer to WordPress as a content management system (CMS), and with the addition of the Front Page Displays setting (**Figure 5.18**), this characterization is truer now than it's ever been.

Figure 5.18 WordPress isn't limited to displaying a list of posts on your home page. You can set it to display a static page as well.

The traditional WordPress installation simply displays a list of the most recent posts on the index page (the first page people see when they navigate to your blog), and that's still the default setting.

Selecting a static page as your front page, however, opens some interesting possibilities. You can create a page that provides static information about you or your product (as I discuss in Chapter 8), which makes your blog look more like a traditional Web site.

You can also designate a page as a Posts page, which lists your blog posts separately. So when people visit your blog's index page, they see a page full of whatever information you want to give them, with a link to another page that is, for all intents and purposes, your blog. This option makes it a breeze to create a dynamic site with content that's easy to update.

If you decide to set up your blog in this manner, but you don't see any pages listed in the Front Page and Posts Page drop-down menus, there's a simple explanation: You have to create the pages before you complete these settings.

No matter where you decide to list your posts, whether it be on the index page or on a subpage, you have the option of showing as many or as few posts as you want. Just type the number in the Blog Pages Show at Most text box (**Figure 5.19**). Some blogs are well suited to showing a single post on a page at a time (videoblogs or photoblogs, for example); others benefit from more posts per page (such as a links blog).

 tip   The more posts you have on a page, the longer that page will take to load, which may be a consideration if you have many readers who come to your site without a broadband connection.

Figure 5.19 This setting controls how many blog posts are displayed per page.

Configuring your feeds

Blogs probably wouldn't be as popular as they are without syndication feeds. These feeds are actually text files formatted in such as a way as to make them easily parsed by clients called *feed readers* or *RSS readers*. If you think of your blog as a magazine, your feed is a way for readers to subscribe to your publication. Just as the editor of a magazine has to decide what to publish, you have to decide what information to include in your feeds. Remember that feeds are important to a blog; a good feed is one that makes people want to keep reading.

Number of posts

The first decision you have to make is how many posts to include in the feed. This setting is important when a person first subscribes to your feed, because it determines how many posts he gets right off the bat. The default setting, 10 (**Figure 5.20**), is a good number in my opinion—just enough to get someone up to speed on your posts and not enough to overwhelm him.

Syndication feeds show the most recent	10 posts
For each article in a feed, show	⦿ Full text ◯ Summary
Encoding for pages and feeds	UTF-8 The character encoding you write your blog in (UTF-8 is recommended)

Figure 5.20 Options for your blog's feed.

Feed content

The second decision is much more basic: How much content do you want to provide in your feed? You have to keep in mind that people who subscribe to your blog's feed are reading it in their feed readers, not by loading your Web site. As a result, they won't see any ads that you may have on your site, which makes some site owners nervous. You can give subscribers just a taste of your post and force them to visit your site to read the whole thing by selecting the Summary radio button (refer to Figure 5.20).

I think this method is foolish, however, for a couple of reasons:

- If someone has gone to the trouble of subscribing to your blog, she's a pretty big fan of your work. Why punish her zeal by making her click a link to read all your wisdom?

- People who use feed readers are pretty Web-savvy, which means that they aren't likely to click an ad and trap to zap the monkey. You won't be making any money off them with your ads anyway, so you should make it as easy as possible for them to read your stuff in the hope that they'll share it with their friends (who may be more inclined to zap the monkey).

So I recommend that you accept the default setting, Full Text. You'll thank me later. I also suggest that you accept the default encoding for pages and feeds (refer to Figure 5.20).

Discussion Settings

I've covered settings that govern how you post to your blog and how people read your blog, so what's left? Commenting, of course. Most of the options that you find in the Discussion tab are designed to reduce comment spam, allowing you to set a few simple parameters that apply to all comments on your blog.

Default article settings

The options in the Default Article Settings section apply to all of your posts, and as you see in **Figure 5.21**, they're all enabled when you install WordPress.

Figure 5.21 Article defaults are oddly named but useful.

Here's what the three options mean:

- **Attempt to Notify Any Blogs Linked to from the Article (Slows Down Posting).** When you link to a blog post, WordPress attempts to notify the recipient of the link so that he can track who's linking to his post. This notification is known as a *pingback*. Then the linked blog can be configured to list all pingbacks (as well as *trackbacks*, which are basically the same) on a given post, thereby linking to your post on the post you linked to.

  Why would you want to turn this option off? As the setting's name itself notes, it slows posting slightly (though I've noticed hardly any slowness). The main reason for clearing this check box is to keep your blog private, if you don't want to broadcast to the world the fact that you're blogging.

- **Allow Link Notifications from Other Blogs (Pingbacks and Trackbacks).** This features tells your blog to accept, and display, the trackbacks and pingbacks that other blogs send to your blog.

 note If you decide to send out pingbacks, you should also accept them (which is only polite!).

- **Allow People to Post Comments on the Article.** This setting enables or disables comments on posts at the system level. Out of the gate, WordPress assumes that you want people to comment on your posts, so it enables comments. If you'd rather not deal with comments, simply clear this check box.

  No matter what you set here, you also have the option of enabling or disabling comments on a per-post basis.

Notification options

Now the e-mail address you entered earlier comes into play (refer to "E-mail address" earlier in this chapter). No doubt you'll be interested to know when people post a comment on something you wrote. You can direct WordPress to e-mail you, the administrator, each and every time someone comments on any post, as well as every time a comment is awaiting moderation (which I discuss later in this chapter).

Choose one of the E-Mail Me Whenever options (**Figure 5.22**) to be notified when:

- **Anyone Posts a Comment.** Every comment on your blog, whether or not it's about a post you wrote, is e-mailed to you because you're the blog's administrator. This feature is great for keeping track of discussions on your blog, but if your blog starts getting a serious amount of comments, your inbox can get overwhelmed quickly.

- **A Comment Is Held for Moderation.** Another weapon against comment spam is comment moderation, which keeps all new incoming comments in a virtual holding pen. A comment can't be published on your blog until a user of your blog who plays the proper role logs in and approves it manually. (See Chapter 3 for more info on user roles.) If you enable this option, you get an e-mail about every comment that's waiting for moderation and won't forget to approve legitimate comments. (Almost nothing is worse than commenting on someone's blog and never seeing that comment published.)

Figure 5.22 WordPress can keep you in the loop about comments.

Comment management

You can set some ground rules for comments in the next section of the Discussion tab: Before a Comment Appears (**Figure 5.23**). These options make managing comments a little easier by giving some comments a pass out of moderation (which means that they're posted without intervention by you or a designated user).

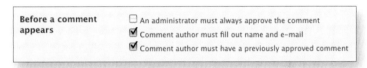

Figure 5.23 Comment spam is no fun, which is why you can set some minimum requirements for comments.

You can set any of these options:

- **An Administrator Must Always Approve the Comment.** You'll notice that this option isn't enabled by default. Who wants to spend all her time approving comments? But if you're a control freak, you can simply check this check box to make sure that no comments can on your blog without your approval.

- **Comment Author Must Fill out Name and E-Mail.** It's very easy to be anonymous on the Internet, and when people don't need to take responsibility for their actions, they do things that they'd normally never do, such as leave nasty comments on nice people's blogs (which has happened to me!). Forcing people to fill in a name and e-mail address makes them think about leaving a harsh comment, even if they simply comment under a fake name and e-mail address. If you want to allow anonymous commenters, clear this check box.

- **Comment Author Must Have a Previously Approved Comment.** Rewarding good behavior is a tenet of our society, and the same holds true in WordPress. This option works on the theory that someone who had a previous comment approved by an administrator has earned the right to leave comments without moderation.

  If you enable this option, as soon as a preapproved commenter leaves another comment, it appears on the blog. This arrangement not only makes your commenter feel good, but also means that you have to spend less time moderating comments—and that's a good thing, as one famous blogger might say. (Yes, Martha Stewart has a blog, and she even runs WordPress.)

Comment moderation

I've mentioned comment moderation a few times already, and now I can give you a tour of the section that controls how comments end up in the moderation queue. Your blog is your kingdom, and you can rule it as you like (feel the power flow through you!). Setting a few options in the Comment Moderation section (**Figure 5.24**) helps you fight the scourge of comment spam.

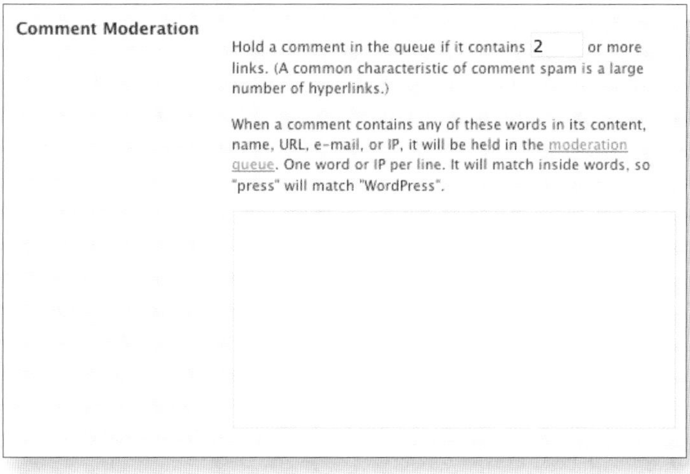

Figure 5.24 Comment moderation is another line of defense against comment spam.

By default, a comment that has two or more links in it is held for moderation, even if the commenter in question is preapproved to leave comments (refer to the preceding section, "Comment management"). Why do this? Most comment spam contains a large number of links, usually to porn sites, which you probably aren't going to want on your blog. If you think legitimate users will be leaving more than two links in the body of their comments ,you can adjust the number to your liking.

The large text box in this section lets you define some criteria that land a comment in moderation, no matter who leaves it. You can list words, IP (Internet Protocol) addresses, or particular links —one per line. If the terms you enter here appear in the name, e-mail, URL, or text section of a comment, that comment is held in the moderation queue to wait for approval (or disapproval, as the case may be).

Comment blacklist

One step beyond comment moderation is the *comment blacklist*. To use this feature, just enter a list of banned items (such as URLs, IP addresses, terms, and e-mail addresses) in the Comment Blacklist section (**Figure 5.25**). When any of these items is used in a comment, WordPress marks that comment as spam. Any comment that's marked as spam doesn't appear on your blog or even go into the moderation queue; it's held in your blog's spam queue, which is just like the Junk Mail folder in your e-mail account.

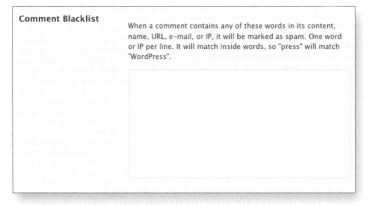

Figure 5.25 The time will come when you'll want to ban certain things, and the Comment Blacklist section is where you do that.

By default, WordPress doesn't give you a way to see what comments are in the spam queue. But if you activate the Akismet spam plug-in (see Chapter 10), you unlock several options related to spam comments that help you fight spam.

Avatar Settings

WordPress.org, along with WordPress.com, supports the Gravatar service. *Gravatar* (Globally Recognized Avatars) is yet another central service that complements WordPress (and is another offering from Automattic).

Knowing your avatars from your gravatars

In case you aren't familiar with the concept on which this service is based, you need to start by getting familiar with avatars. An *avatar* is a digital artifact, such as a small picture, that represents you in cyber-space. Gravatar takes this concept one step further by allowing you to associate an avatar with an e-mail address—thereby creating a *gravatar*. Whenever you comment from that e-mail address on a blog that supports gravatars, your little icon shows up (**Figure 5.26**).

Figure 5.26 The author's gravatar. Handsome devil, ain't he?

 tip   If you're interested in learning more about gravatars or setting up one for yourself, check out the Gravatar Web site: www.gravatar.com.

Enabling and disabling avatars

I'm willing to wager that gravatars are among those things that inspire strong feelings, both for and against. Some people think that gravatars liven up a drab blog and let people express their individuality; others think gravatars are a silly waste of time. WordPress can accommodate either viewpoint. You can enable or disable gravatars with one click.

If you don't want them on your blog, select the Don't Show Avatars radio button in the Avatar Display section (**Figure 5.27**), and skip to "Privacy Settings" later in this chapter.

Avatar Display	○ Don't show Avatars
	◉ Show Avatars

Figure 5.27 Avatars aren't for everyone.

Setting a default avatar

I know what you're thinking: "Scott, you have a great avatar!" Thanks— you're too kind. But what about folks who don't have avatars of their own? You can set a default avatar that WordPress will display for anyone who doesn't have a personal avatar. **Figure 5.28** shows the options in the Default Avatar section:

- Static images (Mystery Man and the Gravatar logo)

- Nothing at all (Blank)

- Avatars that WordPress generates randomly, based on the user's e-mail address: Identicon (which looks like a bar code), Wavatar (a face based on a random geometric shape), or MonsterID (a little monster).

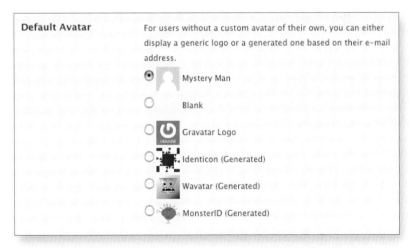

Figure 5.28 Not everyone has an avatar, so you can set a default avatar for those who aren't hip to the scene.

Avatar Ratings

Allowing people to post random pictures to your blog, even if they're in the form of tiny avatars, can be risky. A picture that one person thinks is appropriate may offend someone else. That's why WordPress has a rating system for avatars that follows the familiar U.S. movie rating system (**Figure 5.29**).

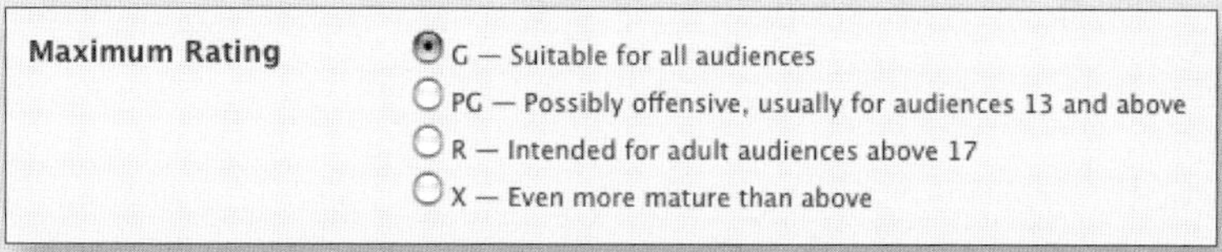

Maximum Rating
- ⦿ G — Suitable for all audiences
- ◯ PG — Possibly offensive, usually for audiences 13 and above
- ◯ R — Intended for adult audiences above 17
- ◯ X — Even more mature than above

Figure 5.29 If you don't want racy avatars on your blog, select the G radio button.

The ratings break down this way:

- G: family friendly

- PG: appropriate for people 13 and older

- R: intended for mature audiences

- X: anything goes!

Unlike movie ratings, which are assigned by a governing board, avatar ratings are assigned by the very same person who created the avatar in the first place. The default rating is G. If you're open to having racier avatars gracing your blog, you can set this rating higher. (Don't worry—you can always change your mind later.)

Privacy Settings

Think back to when you installed WordPress (lo, these many pages ago; flip back to Chapter 2). Do you recall that the installer asked you whether you wanted your blog to be listed with search engines (such as Google)? If you ever change your mind about that choice, you can easily toggle the Blog Visibility setting (**Figure 5.30**).

Figure 5.30 Search engines aren't all-seeing. You can opt out of them by making your blog "invisible."

note   Blocking search engines won't stop people from loading your blog; they just won't be able to find it easily.

Permalink Settings

The Internet is built on the concept of linking. You link to my blog, I link to yours, and everyone's happy. The unspoken agreement in linking is that the link location won't change. Each of your individual posts has a URL associated with it; this URL is called a *permalink*. This permalink is meant to be permanent so that people can always find your post, no matter when they visit that link.

Structure of a permalink

By default, a blog's URL structure looks like this:

`http://www.wordpressforall.com/?p=11`

The first part is the blog's URL (in this example, www.wordpressforall. com). After the slash (/) is ?p=, which is how PHP handles URL variables (in this case, p stands for *post*). The number is the POST ID variable of the post in question. Databases such as MySQL can easily remember things based on variables like POST ID, but we humans are made of different stuff. No one has ever said to me, "Hey, Scott, I really enjoyed Post 243 on your blog the other day."

People aren't the only things that are at a disadvantage with the default WordPress URL structure: The URLs aren't very friendly to search engines. The more descriptive your permalinks are, the better a search engine can index them, resulting in more people being able to find your blog.

Permalinks are important, which is why WordPress devotes a whole section of settings to them. Before I get into the various kinds of permalinks you can set up for your blog, however, I need to discuss how they work on a technical level.

How permalinks work

WordPress supports various types of permalinks by using the `mod_rewrite` module for Apache—a piece of software known as a Web server. Your Web host most likely is using Apache because the software is both very popular and free (funny how that works). Functionality can be added to Apache via modules, one of which is `mod_rewrite`, which enables Apache to rewrite URLs on the fly. This module is important for purposes of this discussion because no matter which permalink structure you choose, WordPress uses the URL with the `POST ID` in it to find your post. The `mod_rewrite` module knows how to map one URL that is easy to remember to another URL based on rules.

The `mod_rewrite` rules can become complicated quickly, but WordPress takes care of writing the rules for you, so don't worry about them. Check your Web host's documentation, however, to make sure that its servers support `mod_rewrite`.

tip If you're interested to see the `mod_rewrite` rules, look for a file called .htaccess. Notice the leading dot, which in many operating systems means that the file is hidden. Check your FTP program's preferences, and make sure that it's set to show you invisible files. Open the file in a text editor, but don't change anything. You wouldn't want to break your blog's URL structure.

Permalink structure options

When you've made sure that `mod_rewrite` is available to you, go ahead and pick your permalink structure (**Figure 5.31**).

⦿ Default	http://www.wordpressforall.com/?p=123
○ Day and name	http://www.wordpressforall.com/2008/08/23/sample-post/
○ Month and name	http://www.wordpressforall.com/2008/08/sample-post/
○ Numeric	http://www.wordpressforall.com/archives/123
○ Custom Structure	

Figure 5.31 The various permalink structures that WordPress offers. You can make a custom structure if none of these suits you.

WordPress has five options for permalinks. I discuss them all in the following sections.

Default

The default structure isn't very friendly, as you see in Figure 5.31.

Day and Name

This option creates a permalink based on a combination of the date of the post and the post title. Suppose that a post called "Wordpress for All launches" was posted August 18, 2008. If you choose the Day and Name option, you get this permalink:

http://www.wordpressforall.com/2008/08/18/wordpress-for-all-launches/

Notice that the title in the link is all lowercase. If I'd used any non-URL-friendly characters such as an apostrophe (') or a percent sign (%) in the title, WordPress would have stripped those characters out so that the link would work in Web browsers.

Month and Name

This option drops the day from the URL for a shorter permalink, such as this:

http://www.wordpressforall.com/2008/08/wordpress-for-all-launches/

 tip Some people like shorter permalinks because they're easier to type.

Numeric

The Numeric option is even shorter, creating a permalink like this:

http://www.wordpressforall.com/archives/11

This permalink structure brings back your old friend `POST ID` but presents it in a way that is a little less cryptic than `?p=11`.

Creating Custom Permalinks

Want to create a few custom permalink structures, just for fun? Sure you do.

If you use the author tag (`%author%`) like so,

`/%author%/%year%/%postname%/`

you get a permalink that features the author's user name, the year, and the post name (and you can add other units of time if you like):

`http://www.wordpressforall.com/scott/2008/wordpress-for-all-launches/`

You don't have to limit yourself to the WordPress tags. Here, I've started my custom structure with the word `permalink`:

`/permalink/%year%/%monthnum%/%postname%/`

That structure generates this permalink:

`http://www.wordpressforall.com/permalink/2008/08/wordpress-for-all-launches/`

You can also add text to the end of tags to add extensions. If you ever plan on migrating your WordPress blog to a series of static HTML files, this permalink will save you some broken links:

`/permalink/%postname%.html`

See that `.html` at the end? It makes the permalink look like this:

`http://www.wordpressforall.com/permalink/wordpress-for-all-launches.html`

WordPress is still building this page dynamically, but now you have the option of creating a static HTML version of this page, and links won't break. Nifty, huh?

Custom Structure

Whenever you select one of the first four permalink structures, the Custom Structure text box is populated automatically. When you select Day and Name, for example, this appears in the text box:

/%year%/%monthnum%/%day%/%postname%/

All permalink structures are built from these permalink tags. You can build your very own custom permalink structure (see the nearby sidebar) by mixing and matching tags.

 tip For a full list of tags that you can use in your WordPress permalink structure, visit this page of the WordPress Codex: http://codex. wordpress.org/Using_Permalinks#Structure_Tags.

Category and tag permalinks

You have two ways to organize your content in WordPress: tags and categories. I get into the differences between the two in Chapter 6, but suffice it to say that both options exist. You can change the way the permalinks associated with categories and tags work by setting their *base phrase*—a word that's used after your blog's URL in the tag/category URL as the foundation for the link.

By default, the permalink that lists all posts categorized as wordpress on my blog looks like this:

http://www.wordpressforall.com/category/wordpress/

Similarly, the permalink for anything tagged blogging looks like this:

http://www.wordpressforall.com/tag/blogging/

If you leave the Category Base and Tag Base text boxes blank (**Figure 5.32**), WordPress uses these defaults.

Category base	
Tag base	

Figure 5.32 Categories and tags also have permalinks, and you can change their base phrases here.

If you want your categories to be called subjects instead, however, type **subject** in the Category Base text box and click Save. Now the permalink looks like this:

```
http://www.wordpressforall.com/subject/wordpress/
```

You can mix and match default tag bases and custom category bases with no problem.

Miscellaneous Settings

These settings are the oddballs in the lot. They don't fit anywhere else, so they congregate together in the miscellaneous section (who knew that settings could be like high school?). More often than not, these settings don't have to be changed from their defaults, but take a look at them and decide for yourself.

Uploads management

No doubt you'll be uploading lots of files to WordPress when you write posts. These files can include pictures, movies, and music, to name just a few.

Uploads folder and file path

By default, WordPress stores the files you upload in the following directory: wp-content/uploads. In **Figure 5.33**, however, the value for the uploads folder is much longer because I have other Web sites on the same service that hosts my WordPress blog. The full directory has been appended.

Store uploads in this folder	/home/.embrown/smcnulty/wordpressforall.
	Default is wp-content/uploads
Full URL path to files (optional)	
☑ Organize my uploads into month- and year-based folders	

Figure 5.33 WordPress needs to know where to keep uploaded files and how you want them organized.

If you want to store files in a different location, just type it in the Store Uploads in This Folder text box. When you do, the Full URL Path to Files setting is no longer optional; WordPress no longer knows where the files are stored, so you need to fill in the URL so that files will show up.

 If you moved your WordPress files to a different directory from your blog, check to make sure that the default uploads-folder location is correct. If it still points to the original location of your WordPress installation, your uploaded files won't show up.

Suppose that I want to store my files in a directory called files. I'd type **files** in the Store Uploads in This Folder text box and set the Full URL path to **http://www.wordpressforall.com/files/**.

Uploads organization

After you've been blogging for a while, you'll amass a large collection of random files on your server. WordPress organizes all uploaded files in monthly and annual folders.

Suppose that on August 12, 2008, you uploaded a file called scott.gif. WordPress checks your uploads folder for that file. If a folder called 2008 doesn't exist, WordPress creates it, as well as a folder called 08, which it places inside the 2008 folder. Then it places the image you uploaded inside the 08 folder. The URL for this image would be something like this:

http://www.wordpressforall.com/files/2008/08/scott.gif

If you prefer, you can clear the organization check box (refer to Figure 5.33) to keep your files as messy as you like.

Image sizes

Whenever you upload a picture to WordPress, a couple of things happen:

- The file is saved in the appropriate directory. (If the directory doesn't exist, WordPress creates it.)

- Two thumbnails are created: a small one and a medium one.

The Thumbnail Size and Medium Size settings (**Figure 5.34**) allow you to tell WordPress how large these thumbnails should be.

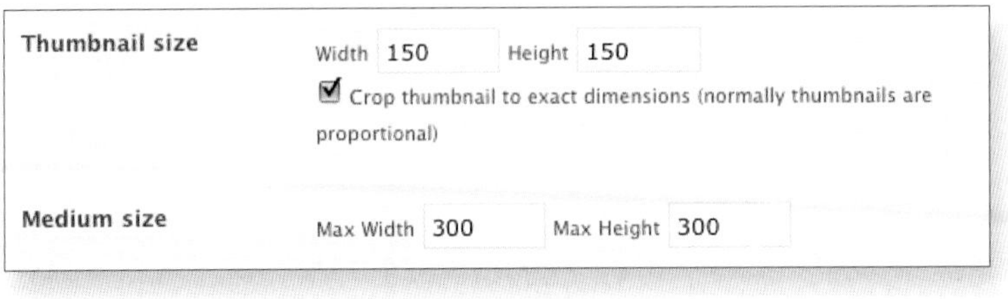

Thumbnail size	
	Width 150 Height 150
	☑ Crop thumbnail to exact dimensions (normally thumbnails are proportional)
Medium size	
	Max Width 300 Max Height 300

Figure 5.34 Thumbnail sizes are set systemwide.

The Crop Thumbnail to Exact Dimensions option, when enabled, means that the cropped thumbnail will have the exact dimensions you set in the Width and Height text boxes. (By default, thumbnails are 150 by 150 pixels.) If you don't want a square thumbnail, clear this check box and enter the width and height values you prefer.

These settings come into play when you're inserting an image into a post. You have the choice of inserting the original picture or one of the two thumbnails that WordPress creates based on these settings.

Miscellaneous miscellaneous settings

In addition to posts and pages, you can create links with your WordPress blog. When you check the Track Links' Update Times check box (**Figure 5.35**), your blog connects with a third party server (Ping-o-Matic; refer to "Update services" earlier in this chapter) to see whether the linked sites have been updated. You can use this feature to create a *blogroll* (a list of links to blogs that you enjoy) that shows the last time the blog was updated.

☐ Track Links' Update Times

☐ Use legacy `my-hacks.php` file support

Figure 5.35 Two seldom-used miscellaneous settings.

Support for the my-hacks.php file is a legacy feature of WordPress, and chances are that you won't be using this file, which allowed users to change the design and functionality of their blogs at system level before WordPress supported plug-ins.

6

Preparing to Post

Building a good blog post is all about having good content. WordPress won't make you a good blogger, but if you know how to format your post, you can at least appear to know what you're doing. (I've been coasting along using this strategy for most of my life.) In this chapter, I show you how to set up a WordPress post like a pro, but I leave the actual content up to you.

WordPress tries to get out of your way so as to make writing posts easy. The Write tab is the first link in the navigation bar at the top of every WordPress admin page (right below your blog's title). When you click the Write tab (**Figure 6.1** on the next page), WordPress displays the Post panel.

| Write | Manage | Design | Comments |
| Post | Page | Link | |

Figure 6.1 The Write tab allows you to write posts, pages, or links.

From this tab, you can create any of the three content types:

- **Post.** When you think of a blog, you probably think of posts. These entries make up the bulk of a blog's content.

- **Page.** Pages share many features with posts but are used for slightly different things. Pages are made of content that is more static than posts. "About" pages and contact pages are great examples.

- **Link.** If you're interested in having a list of links to various Web sites, the Links panel is where you create it. You can categorize links and display them on your blog. A good example is the blogroll, which graces many a blog out there.

 tip One of the first things you see when you log in to the admin section of your blog is the orange Right Now link bar. At the far-right end of that bar, you see two links: Write a Post and Write a Page. Click either link to start writing a post or page.

In this chapter, I discuss posts. I make my way through the rest of the content types in the following chapters. The three content types share many concepts, and I won't be repeating them in each chapter. To save everyone some time, I'll just highlight the differences.

Breaking Down the Elements of a Post

No matter what blogging system you use, posts always have three elements: a title, a body, and an author. WordPress adds a few more things to the mix, but the basics are the same. The rest of this chapter goes through the various sections of the Post panel in order.

Title

Titles are like headlines in a newspaper. A good title makes you want to read the post, makes you curious, and gives you a sense of what you're about to read. Depending on your permalink structure, your titles may also be used in the permalinks themselves. (Refer to Chapter 5 for more info on permalinks.)

As you write a post, WordPress automatically saves at certain intervals to ensure that if your browser crashes or you're somehow disconnected from WordPress, your entire post isn't lost. The permalink for your post is generated after the first automatic save. Right below the title you see, in a light font, the word *Permalink* followed by the URL of the permalink (**Figure 6.2**). The last section of the permalink is highlighted. This part, called the *slug*, generally is based on the title of the post.

Title

Latin blogging for fun

Permalink: http://www.wordpressforall.com/2008/08/28/latin-blogging-for-fun/ Edit

Figure 6.2 A very creative title for a blog post, don't you think? Notice the permalink below the title.

If you don't like the slug, just click the Edit link; change the slug displayed in the text box (**Figure 6.3**) to something you do like; and click Save. Now you have an improved permalink that says exactly what you want.

Permalink: http://www.wordpressforall.com/2008/08/28/ latin-blogging-for-fun   Save Cancel

Figure 6.3 Editing a post's permalink is easy.

note   Titles, like all other fields in a post, are optional.

Body

The meat of posting happens in the body, which you write in the Post panel. You have lots of options in this panel, and you can use as many or as few of them as you like. (One great thing about WordPress is that it offers loads of features but doesn't force you to use them.)

When you use the Post panel, you can choose either of two options at the right end of the title bar:

- **Visual.** Click this tab to write your posts with the Visual Editor.

- **HTML.** Click this tab to write in straight HTML code.

You can switch back and forth between the two options easily. The Visual and HTML areas have different features, so I look at them separately in the following sections.

Composing and Formatting a Post

Writing is a very personal activity, and every writer has a list of particular tools, pens, notebooks, and the like that he prefers. Writing in your WordPress blog is just like jotting something down in your favorite notebook, except that you have no notebook, and you aren't actually committing ink (or graphite) to paper. WordPress gives you two different ways to interact with the Post panel: the Visual Editor and HTML view. Both features allow you to write and format a post—just in different ways. Choose whichever feature you're more comfortable with.

Writing with the Visual Editor

WordPress uses an open-source visual HTML editor called *TinyMCE*. All the features listed in this section are available in any product that uses TinyMCE.

 note You can find out more about this JavaScript marvel by visiting the TinyMCE Web site (http://tinymce.moxiecode.com).

The Visual Editor (**Figure 6.4**) takes care of all the code behind the formatting of your words. If you're not interested in learning how to hand-code

HTML, you'll want to use this editor to post to your blog. The following sections cover the Visual Editor's buttons and show you what they do.

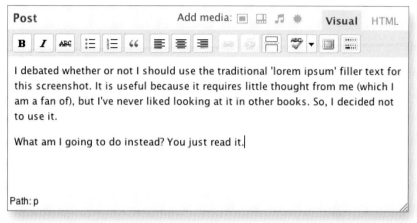

Figure 6.4 Composing a post in the Visual Editor.

> **tip** When you hover your mouse pointer over a button in the Visual Editor, a tool tip pops up, displaying the keyboard shortcut for that button.

Formatting toolbars: Top row

No matter which view you use, you'll see a toolbar at the top of the editing form. Each toolbar button formats your post in one way or another. This section covers the top toolbar.

B Sometimes you want a word or phrase to stand out, and one of the best ways to achieve that goal is to boldface that text. Select whatever words you want to boldface; then click the Bold button. The selected words will be bold in the editor window and in the post as well.

I Italics are another way of emphasizing your words, and as you might guess, the Italic button applies that format. Select the words you want to italicize, click the button, and you're done.

ABC The Strikethrough button is a great way to acknowledge a mistake without removing the erroneous information. ~~My face~~ Strikethrough is also used for comedic effect in many cases.

The next two buttons let you create lists. To create a bulleted list (also known as an unordered list), click the leftmost of these two buttons; then select some text or an image to be your first list item. WordPress inserts a bullet, and when you press Enter or Return, you can add another item to the list. (Pressing Enter or Return twice ends the list so you can go back to writing normally.) A numbered (or ordered) list works the same way but creates a list whose items are numbered (as you may have suspected from the name).

Quoting people is fairly common in the blogosphere, but how do you note that the relevant section of your post is a quote from elsewhere? Block quotes are the answer. When you select some text and click the Block Quote button, WordPress creates a block quote and populates it with the selected text. Depending on the styling of your blog, block quotes can appear in a variety of ways. Usually, a block quote is indented and shown with a different-colored background, so that there's no doubt in the reader's mind that this section is a quote. (Always credit your sources, kids. No one likes a plagiarist.)

The next three buttons—Left, Center, and Right—allow you to align the text of your post. You can use whichever option you want, but WordPress defaults to left-aligned text.

I'll wager you'll use this set of buttons the most. The button with the three links of chain on it turns any selected word or phrase into a hyperlink. Clicking this button brings up the Insert/Edit Link dialog box (**Figure 6.5**), where you set the following options:

- **Link URL.** The destination of the link (a URL of some kind).

- **Target.** The target setting specifies where the link opens in the user's Web browser. You can have the link open in the same browser window or a new one.

- **Title.** The title of the link, which shows up when someone hovers a mouse pointer over the link or accesses your site with a text browser.

- **Class.** Class is a styling option that can be used, in conjunction with some CSS, to apply formatting to your links. If you don't know what CSS is, chances are that you can ignore this option.

Figure 6.5 The Insert/Edit Link dialog box allows you to insert a new link or edit an existing one.

If you want to change any of these values for an existing link, click the Hyperlink button again; the dialog box shows you the current values, and you can change them however you want.

Back in the Visual Editor toolbar, click the button with the broken chain link to remove the linking code from the selected word. The word itself isn't deleted—just the code that makes it a link.

It's commonplace to see a Read More link at the bottom of blog posts nowadays. The idea is that you should cut longer blog posts into two sections so that your blog's front page isn't overwhelmed by your epic post about Bayesian economics and its effect on lobster prices in central Utah. Clicking this button inserts a `<!--more-->` quicktag and displays a dotted line across the posting field in the Post panel. Anything before the dotted line is displayed on the front page of your blog. At the end of that section is a Read More link. Clicking the Read More link takes you to the entries page, which contains the full text of the post (including everything after the dotted line in the Post panel).

I don't know about you, but spell checkers have ruined what little spelling ability I have (just ask my editors). WordPress furthers my spelling decline by offering spell check. Clicking the Spell Check button enables it; clicking the button again disables it. Misspelled words are underlined in red; click an underlined word to see a list of suggested spellings, as well as options to ignore this occurrence of the word or all occurrences in the entire post.

Full-screen mode is all the rage with desktop word processors. It allows you to block out all distractions and concentrate on the work at hand: crafting memorable words for your readers. The Full Screen button expands the Post panel's posting field to occupy your entire screen. Click the button again to toggle back to normal view.

The very last button is interesting, because it isn't the last button at all. Clicking the "kitchen sink" button (yes, that's the real name) reveals a second toolbar that's hidden from view by default (**Figure 6.6**).

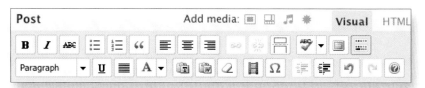

Figure 6.6 The second toolbar is usually hidden away. Clicking the kitchen-sink button reveals it.

Formatting toolbars: Bottom row

This second toolbar offers some functionality that you probably won't need for every post but that may come in handy from time to time. WordPress remembers whether you've displayed this extra toolbar, so if you find yourself using one of these features, you can keep the toolbar on display.

Here are the buttons and what they do:

The Format drop-down menu gives you access to various text-formatting options. Select the text you want to format and choose an option from the drop-down menu: Paragraph, Preformatted, a variety of heading options, and so on.

Because links are traditionally underlined, people avoid underlining text for any other reason. That being said, you can click this button to underline selected text.

Justified text isn't too common on the Web, but if you want all your lines to be the same width, select the text and click this button.

By default, your blog's theme (see Chapter 11) determines the color of the text in your posts. If you want to change the color of selected text, this button gives you access to all the colors of the rainbow. Click the down arrow on the button to display a grid of colors (**Figure 6.7**).

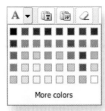

Figure 6.7 You have a full range of colors at your fingertips.

If these choices aren't enough, view even more color options by clicking More Colors at the bottom of the grid. The More Colors panel gives you three options for finding just the right color: Color Picker, which shows a rainbow of colors that you can choose among; Palette, which offers up an expanded grid of colors; and Named, which gives you the opportunity to choose one of the so-called Web-safe colors. Each option displays the hex code for the selected color. (*Hex codes* are used in HTML to tell Web browsers what color to display.) If you know the hex code of the color you're after, you can enter it directly in the box labeled Color.

Copying and pasting text usually is straightforward, but sometimes when you copy text, you also copy unwanted formatting. Click the Paste As Plain Text button to strip out all the formatting and paste only the text. Paste the text in the dialog box that pops up after you click the button (**Figure 6.8**), check or clear the Keep Linebreaks check box, and then click the Insert button to paste the text into your post.

Figure 6.8 The Paste As Plain Text dialog box.

The Paste from Word button also displays a dialog box for your pasted text (**Figure 6.9**). It works the same way as the Paste As Plain Text dialog box (see the preceding paragraph), but instead of stripping out Microsoft Word formatting, it makes that formatting HTML friendly. This feature is very useful if you compose your posts in Word with lots of text formatting and don't want to delete the Word-specific markup that gets copied along with your text.

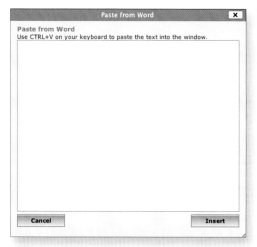

Figure 6.9 The Paste from Word dialog box.

The Remove Formatting button strips all formatting out of the selected text.

The Insert/Edit Embedded Media button deals specifically with media files (QuickTime, Adobe Flash, Windows Media, and Real Media files) that you want to embed in your post. The various options for each file type are beyond the scope of this book; I recommend that you poke around the Advanced tab of the media panel and see what works best for you.

Custom characters (also known as *special characters* and *HTML entities*) are characters that have special HTML codes associated with them to ensure that they show up correctly in Web browsers. Click this button to open the Select Custom Character dialog box (**Figure 6.10**); then select the character you're interested in to insert it into your post, all without having to worry about the code.

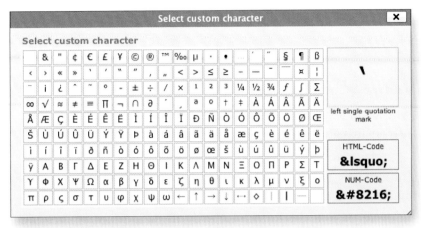

Figure 6.10 The custom-character picker.

The Indent and Outdent buttons indent and outdent paragraphs, respectively. Position the insertion point where you want to apply the formatting, and click the appropriate button.

The Undo button allows you to undo an action such as deleting a word or pasting the wrong text. If you decide that you really did like the post the way it was before, click the Redo button. Your post is as it was.

The Help button displays the help files for the Visual Editor. These files (which include a full list of keyboard shortcuts) should answer most of your questions. If you still have questions, check out the WordPress Codex (http://codex.wordpress.org).

Writing in HTML view

You may want to use HTML view instead when you write your posts, for a couple of reasons:

- You're faster at hand-coding than you are at selecting text and clicking formatting buttons.

- You want to enter some code from a third-party Web site (such as Digg or YouTube).

Any code that you enter in a post via the Visual Editor is treated as text, not as code. This means that the code is displayed just as you entered it—but doesn't execute and call up a video or what have you. Solving this problem is simple: Just click the HTML tab in the Post panel (**Figure 6.11**) and paste your code in the resulting HTML window.

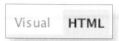

Figure 6.11 Switching between the Visual Editor and HTML view is as simple as clicking a tab.

HTML view allows you to enter code by hand, but it also has a row of buttons that generate code for you (to save time). This view offers some, but not all, of the Visual Editor's functionality. A big difference is that you don't need to select text for the buttons in HTML view to work. Because the buttons in HTML view enter HTML code, which is tag based, clicking a button inserts the appropriate opening tag into the entry. Click the button again to insert the closing tag at the insertion-point location in the post.

Here are the HTML view buttons and what they do:

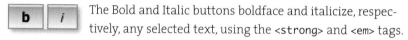

The Bold and Italic buttons boldface and italicize, respectively, any selected text, using the `<strong>` and `<em>` tags.

The Link button creates a link, using the selected word as the link's text. When you click this button, a window pops up; enter the appropriate URL in this window, and you're good to go.

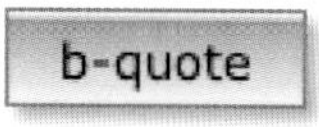

The B-Quote button is the Block Quote button; it does the same thing as its counterpart in the Visual Editor (refer to "Formatting toolbars: Top row" earlier in this chapter).

The Del and Ins buttons flag text that has been deleted from your post or added to your post, respectively. Text between the `<del>` tags is displayed in strikethrough; text between the `<ins>` tags looks like a link (depending on the style of your blog).

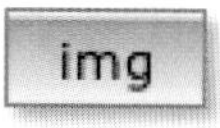

The Img button allows you to insert an image, as long as you know the URL of the image. In "Adding Media to a Post" later in this chapter, though, I cover an easier way to insert images (assuming that they are uploaded to your WordPress blog).

ul ol li The tags that create lists are `<ul>` (unordered, or bulleted), `<ol>` (ordered, or numbered), and `<li>` (list item, used between the `<ul>` or `<ol>` tags). Click the appropriate buttons to insert these tags.

code If you plan on blogging about technical subjects, you'll want to know about the Code button. This button inserts the `<code>` tag, which displays text in a monospace font (`like this`), signifying that it's code of some sort.

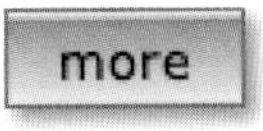

more The More button inserts a Read More link (refer to "Formatting toolbars: Top row" earlier in this chapter). Any text before the `<more>` tag is displayed on the front page of your blog; everything after it appears only on the post's page.

lookup The Lookup button doesn't insert anything into your post. Rather, it looks up the selected word at Answers.com, which can be fun, but I haven't found this particular function to be all that useful.

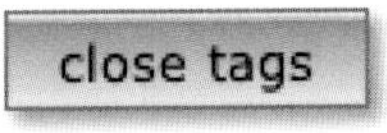

close tags The Close Tags button, as you might expect, closes any open HTML tags. This functionality isn't perfect, though; you should double-check the tags it closes to ensure that they're handled properly.

Adding Media to a Post

A good blog post starts with text, which you now know how to manipulate in WordPress, but also includes other kinds of media. Adding images, movies, audio files, PDFs, and many more media types to your posts is easy and even fun.

You use the Add Media section of the Post panel (**Figure 6.12**) to . . . well, add media to your posts or pages. The four icons represent images, movies, audio files, and all other media files.

Figure 6.12 The Add Media options let you spiffy up your posts with pictures, videos, and other files.

Clicking an icon brings up an appropriate uploader for the media type in question (**Figure 6.13**).

Figure 6.13 Choose a file to upload.

Adding images

The first icon in the Add Media section—the one that looks like a picture frame—adds images to your post. When you click the picture icon, the Choose File page pops up. You can upload a picture (or set of pictures) from your computer or insert a picture from the Web (**Figure 6.14**).

Figure 6.14 Image-upload options include inserting an image from a URL.

I cover both methods in the following sections.

Just Say No to Hotlinking

Insert pictures from the Web with caution. Use this method only for pictures that you own and host yourself or for images that are hosted by a large picture hosting site (such as Flickr).

Posting images from other people's blogs is called *hotlinking* and generally isn't looked upon kindly. Every time someone reads your blog post with a hotlinked picture in it, the person who actually hosts that picture has to pay for the bandwidth your reader uses to view it.

Inserting an image from the Web

If you're sure that you can use this method (refer to the nearby sidebar), you need to provide a few pieces of information:

- **Source.** Enter the URL of the image you want to insert. After you enter something in this text box, WordPress tries to find an image at the URL you provided (assuming that you're connected to the Internet). Depending on what it finds, WordPress displays a green check mark next to the Source text box if the image is reachable or a red X if the image can't be retrieved.

- **Image Title.** The image title, which is required, is used in the TITLE attribute of the image. This attribute is commonly used to describe an element on a Web page, so make sure that your title is appropriate.

- **Image Caption.** A caption serves double duty. Some themes display the text you enter here below the image and also use it to populate the image's `<alt>` tag. (The `<alt>` tag contains the text that you want to show up in the user's browser when the image can't be displayed or the person who's looking at your site is using a text-only browser.)

- **Alignment.** This setting determines how text flows around your image. None causes the image to sit above the text. Left aligns the picture to the left side of the post, and the text flows around it. Center places the image in the center of the post, and text doesn't flow around the image. Right is the opposite of Left.

- **Link URL.** Entering a URL in the Link URL text box turns the picture you're inserting into a link to said URL. You can enter any URL you want in this box or click the Link to Image button, which populates the text box with the URL of the image itself (which will be the same as the Source setting). This feature is useful if you plan to insert a thumbnail of a picture. People can click the thumbnail to see the image at full size.

When you have the settings to your liking (**Figure 6.15**), just click the Insert into Post button. WordPress inserts the image at the location of the insertion point in the post.

Figure 6.15 Notice the check mark next to the Source text box; it means that WordPress found the image.

Uploading an image from your computer

If you want to upload an image from your computer to your blog, which means that you'll be hosting the image on your server, you have to use a WordPress uploader. The default uploader uses the Flash plug-in from Adobe. If you're not a fan of Flash or your browser doesn't support it, you can click the Browser Uploader link at the top of the Choose File page instead. The browser uploader doesn't require plug-ins and should work on most systems.

The Flash uploader has one feature that the browser uploader lacks: a progress bar (**Figure 6.16**). This bar charts the upload process as well as the generation of thumbnails (during which process the progress bar displays the word *Crunching*). You can upload multiple files with either uploader, so if you don't care about the progress bar, either option will suit your needs.

Figure 6.16 The Flash uploader's progress bar may not look like much, but it's very helpful when you're uploading several files.

To upload images from your computer, follow these steps:

1. Click the Choose Files to Upload button (refer to Figure 6.14).

2. Select the photos you want to upload from your local machine.

 tip Holding down the Shift key while you click a bunch of contiguous files allows you to select and upload all those images at the same time. You can also Ctrl-click (or, on the Mac, Control-click) to select noncontiguous files in the same folder.

3. When you have the correct images selected, click Select.

    WordPress starts uploading the files.

When an image is uploaded, the Choose File page displays many of the same settings that it displays for images from the Web, which I cover in the preceding section (**Figure 6.17** on the next page).

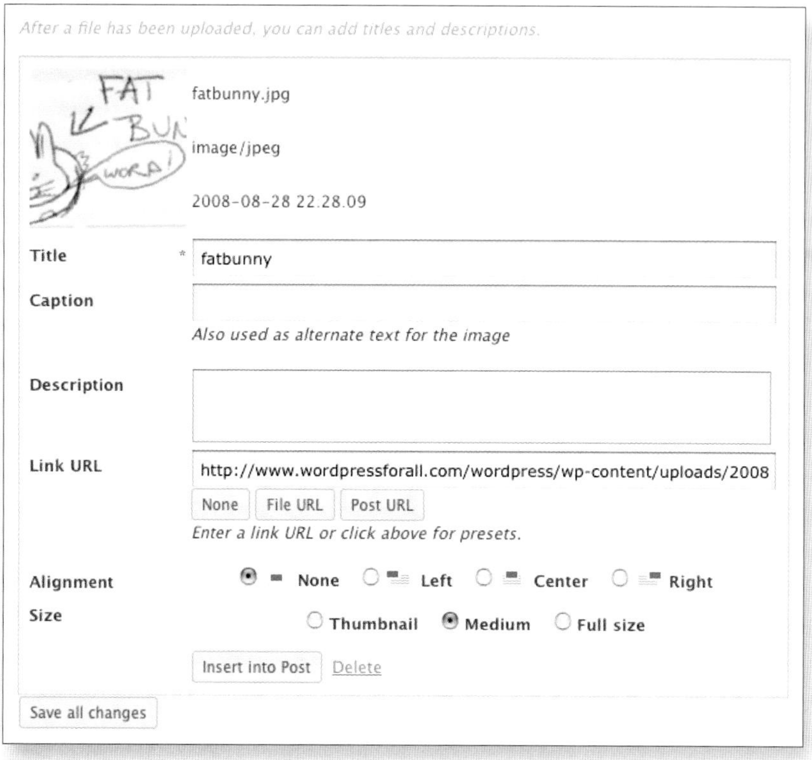

Figure 6.17 After an image has been uploaded from your computer, you can set a few options for it.

Most of the settings do the same things, but here are the differences:

- **Title.** Again, the title is required. This time, in addition to setting the TITLE attribute of this image, the title identifies this image in your blog's Media Library, which I cover in "Using Media Library" later in this chapter.

- **Link URL.** You can set a couple of different options for the link URL: File URL and Post URL.

  File URL allows you to set a direct link to the file on your server. If you upload an image called blogsarecool.jpg, that URL would look like this:

  ```
  http://www.yourblog.com/yourWordPressfolder/wp-content/
  uploads/2008/08/blogsarecool.jpg
  ```

Post URL isn't the permalink of the post itself but a permalink to the image. (For more information on permalinks, flip back to Chapter 5.) When you upload an image to a post, that image is attached to the post, essentially creating a subpost that contains only the uploaded image. The Post URL setting refers to this subpost. This subpost is just like any other post in your blog, in that people can link to it and leave comments. You can click the Post URL button and enter any URL you want to use.

- **Size.** If you're reading the chapters of this book in order, you may recall a setting in Chapter 5 that affects the sizes of thumbnails of uploaded images. This option is where that setting pays off. You can insert the picture at the size of the original (Full Size), or you can insert it as either of two thumbnail options: Thumbnail (the smaller option) or Medium.

tip If, just as you click the Insert into Post button, you realize that the image you're working with isn't right, fear not! You can delete it right from the Choose File page. Click the Delete link, and WordPress warns you that you're about to delete the picture you just uploaded. Click Continue, and the picture is gone.

Working with galleries

Images are associated with the posts in which they are inserted, which allows you to create a gallery of images easily. When you upload multiple files to the same post, you'll notice that the Gallery tab has a number next to it in parentheses (**Figure 6.18**). That number is the number of pictures in a gallery associated with the post. You can insert images individually or insert multiple images as a gallery.

| Choose File | Gallery (7) | Media Library |

Figure 6.18 Image files that are uploaded through a post are attached to that post and automatically added to a gallery.

Why would you want to insert images as a gallery? This method gives you a little more control of how the images are displayed.

In this section, I give you a tour of the Gallery tab.

 note Make sure that you've uploaded at least two images to a post you're working on; otherwise, you won't be able to see the Gallery tab.

Reordering gallery images

Figure 6.19 shows seven pictures associated with a post, listed in the Gallery tab in the order in which they appear in the gallery.

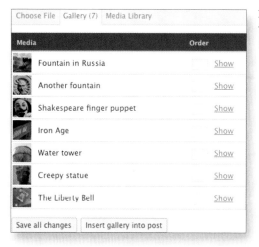

Figure 6.19 The gallery interface lists all the files that have been uploaded to this post.

If you want to change the order, you can do that in either of two ways:

- Click and drag the picture you want to move to a different position. The other pictures move to new places, and the gallery is reordered. Notice that WordPress automatically fills in the Order column after you drop an image in a new position (**Figure 6.20**).

- Setting the Order column by hand also reorders the gallery. Lower numbers appear before higher numbers.

 note If you have an image file that's attached to the post but don't want it to show up in the gallery, leave its Order column blank.

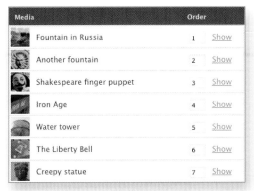

Figure 6.20 If you want to change the order of a picture in the gallery, you can drag the picture or type an new ordinal number in the picture's Order column.

Clicking a Show link (next to the Order column) expands the settings for the selected image (**Figure 6.21**). You can change the title, caption, description, or link URL of the image; you can also insert the image into a post by itself.

Figure 6.21 When you click a Show link in the Gallery tab, you get some options to edit and can insert the file directly into a post.

Click the Save All Changes button at the bottom of the Gallery tab (refer to Figure 6.19) to save both the order and the changes that you made to each image. When your galley is ready to go, click the Insert Gallery into Post button to insert the gallery short code—[gallery]—into your post. This code tells WordPress to display your gallery in that post.

Setting gallery-code options

After all that work, all you get to see in the Post panel is [gallery]? You can set a few options for the short code that aren't available in the gallery interface itself:

- By default, galleries display three images across in each row. You can change this setting by adding columns="x" , where "x" is the number of desired columns. If you want your gallery to have five columns, the code would look like this:

```
[gallery columns="5"]
```

 Keep in mind that your blog's theme may have styling code that works best with a certain number of columns. (I discuss themes in chapters 11 and 12.)

- Galleries automatically show the thumbnails of the images, which makes sense, because you're showing several images in a small space. If you'd rather display one of the other sizes (Medium or Full Size; refer to "Uploading an image from your computer" earlier in this chapter), you can do so by adding size="" to the tag. If you want to show full-size images, use this code:

```
[gallery size="full"]
```

For medium images, use this code:

```
[gallery size="medium"]
```

- Because images that are uploaded to a post are associated with that post, the gallery short code assumes that you want to include the images attached to the post in which the short code is used. If you want to use the same gallery in a different post, but you don't want to upload all those pictures again, you can use the id option.

First, though, you need to know the POST ID of the post associated with the pictures (see the nearby note). After you get the POST ID, enter the short code like so:

```
[galley id="52"]
```

note

The *POST ID* is displayed in the URL of the post form. Just look for *post.php?action=edit&post=52* . The number after the last equal sign is the *POST ID*.

Viewing a gallery on your Web site

After you publish your post, the gallery is live on your site (**Figure 6.22**).

Latin blogging for fun

I debated *whether* or not I should use the traditional 'lorem ipsum' filler text for this screenshot. It is useful because it requires little thought from me (which I am a fan of), but I've never liked looking at it in other books. So, I decided not to it.

What am I going to do instead? You just read it.

Figure 6.22 A post with a gallery, displayed in the default WordPress theme.

Clicking one of the pictures takes you to that picture's page, which shows the picture's title, the medium version of the picture, the description (if it has one), and the next and previous pictures in the gallery (so you can navigate back and forth). Clicking the picture in this page takes you to the full-size version of the picture (**Figure 6.23**).

Figure 6.23
Notice the two pictures at the bottom. Clicking them takes you to the next and previous pictures, respectively.

Editing image settings

You know how to get images into your posts now. But what if you want to change an image's settings? You don't have to delete it and start from scratch. If you move your mouse pointer over an image in a post that you're editing or writing, the two icons shown in **Figure 6.24** appear.

Figure 6.24 Click the landscape icon to edit the picture's settings or the "prohibited" symbol to remove the picture from the post.

The red circle with a line through it—the universal "prohibited" symbol—deletes the image from your post. It doesn't delete the image itself, though; the image still exists in your images folder.

The other icon, which looks like a nice landscape, opens the Edit Image panel (**Figure 6.25**), which gives you access to a host of image settings.

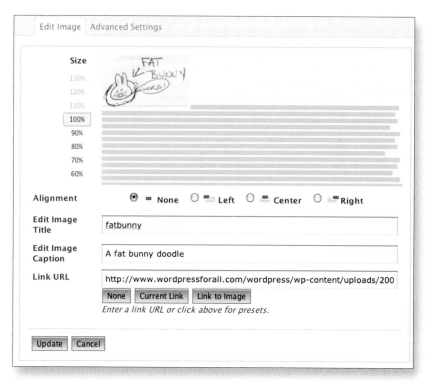

Figure 6.25 Editing an image's settings.

One of the best things about this panel is the simulator section at the top, which shows you what your image is going to look like in the post with the settings that you apply. This preview updates in real time, so you never have to wonder what your changes will do to the final product.

While you're looking at the top section, take note of the Size column, which you can use to adjust the size of the image. Clicking one of the percentage values makes the image smaller (in the case of all values less than 100 percent) or larger (all values greater than 100 percent). Keep in mind that this setting affects the image's appearance; it doesn't make the image file take up any less space. A huge image will still take a while to download, even if you set the size to 60 percent.

I've already covered the rest of the settings in this panel, but it's good to note again that you can change any of them at any time.

Experimenting with advanced image settings

Clicking the Advanced Settings tab brings forth a wonderland of new and exciting (yes, I'm a geek) image settings to play with (**Figure 6.26**).

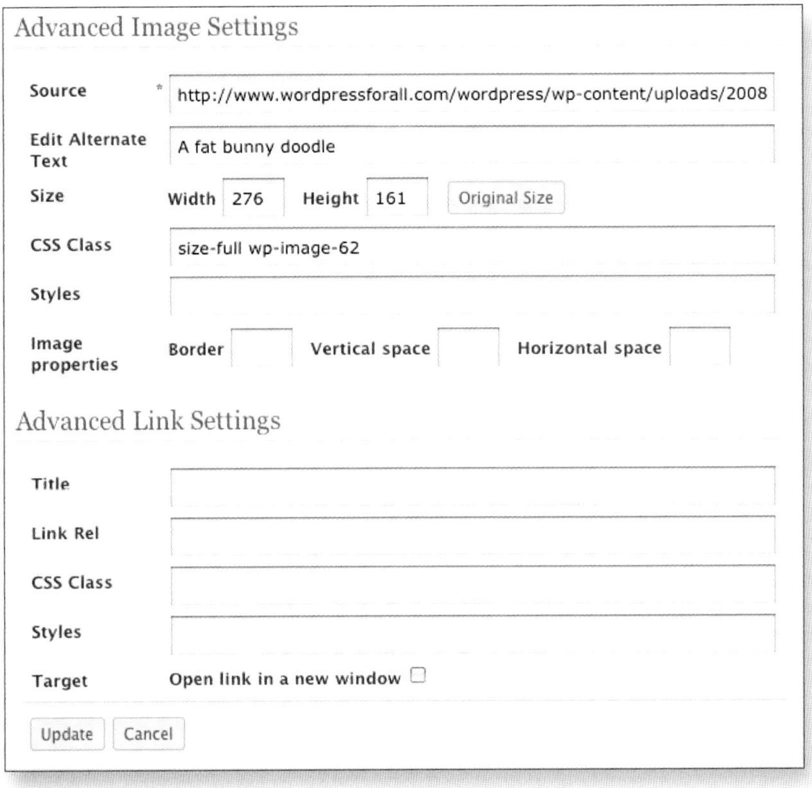

Advanced Image Settings

Source	http://www.wordpressforall.com/wordpress/wp-content/uploads/2008
Edit Alternate Text	A fat bunny doodle
Size	Width 276 Height 161 Original Size
CSS Class	size-full wp-image-62
Styles	
Image properties	Border Vertical space Horizontal space

Advanced Link Settings

Title	
Link Rel	
CSS Class	
Styles	
Target	Open link in a new window ☐

Update   Cancel

Figure 6.26 Advanced image settings are powerful. Don't fiddle with them if you don't know what they do.

Here's what you need to know about the Advanced Image Settings options:

- **Source.** The source of the image is required, and the text box is prepopulated because you've already uploaded this image to your blog. You shouldn't have to change this information unless you recently moved your images to another folder.

- **Edit Alternate Text.** Use this text box to enter the image's <alt> tag (which I discuss in "Inserting an image from the Web" earlier in this chapter).

- **Size.** The Size options control the size of the image. These values are set when you click one of the percentages in the Size column. Don't worry about messing these values up; you can always reset the image to its true size by clicking the Original Size button.

- **CSS Class.** This text box probably will have some value in it. You shouldn't change this value unless you're familiar with the CSS (Cascading Style Sheets) settings of the WordPress theme you're using. (For more info on CSS and themes, see chapters 11 and 12.)

- **Styles.** This setting is another way you can have your site's CSS change how images are displayed. When you enter a value in the Image Properties section (which I talk about next), the Styles text box is populated with a value. WordPress uses CSS itself to control how your images are displayed.

- **Image Properties.** You can enter three values in this section: Border (which puts a black border x pixels wide around the image, where x is the number you enter), Vertical Space, and Horizontal Space. The latter two options values set the amount of horizontal and vertical padding, in pixels, around the image.

When you have all the values set the way you want, make sure to click the Update button to save your settings.

Working with advanced link settings

The Advanced Link Settings section affects the way your image links to itself (or whatever URL you've set it to link to). If the image doesn't link to anything, these settings don't do anything, so you can ignore them.

Here's what you need to know about this group of options:

- **Title.** Enter the title of your link in this text box. This title is what shows up (in certain browsers) when someone hovers a mouse pointer over the link.

- **Link Rel.** This option, short for *Link Relationship,* is a special link property that works with XFN (XHTML Friends Network). It programmatically represents your relationship with the person you are linking to by using commonly agreed-on properties (such as `friend`, `acquaintance`, or `contact`) and the link.

 For more information about XFN and why you may want to start using it, check out its official Web site: http://gmpg.org/xfn.

- **CSS Class** and **Styles.** Like their counterparts in the Advanced Image Settings section, these options affect how your link is displayed, depending on how the CSS of your theme is set up.

- **Target.** By default, the link target is the same browser window. If you want the link to open a separate browser window when it's clicked, check the Open Link in a New Window check box.

Click the Update button to save your settings.

Adding other media types

You may find it odd that I'm lumping together all the other media types when WordPress has a dedicated button for uploading video and audio files and another button for everything else (refer to the Add Media buttons in Figure 6.12 earlier in this chapter). Although it's true that video and audio are separated, the upload process and panel (**Figure 6.27**) are exactly the same whether you're uploading a movie or a PDF file. Inserting media into a post with these buttons simply uploads the media to your wp-content folder and then inserts a link into your post.

When someone clicks that link, her browser displays the media in whatever method is appropriate (downloading the file if it's a PDF or showing it in the proper player if it's a video, for example)

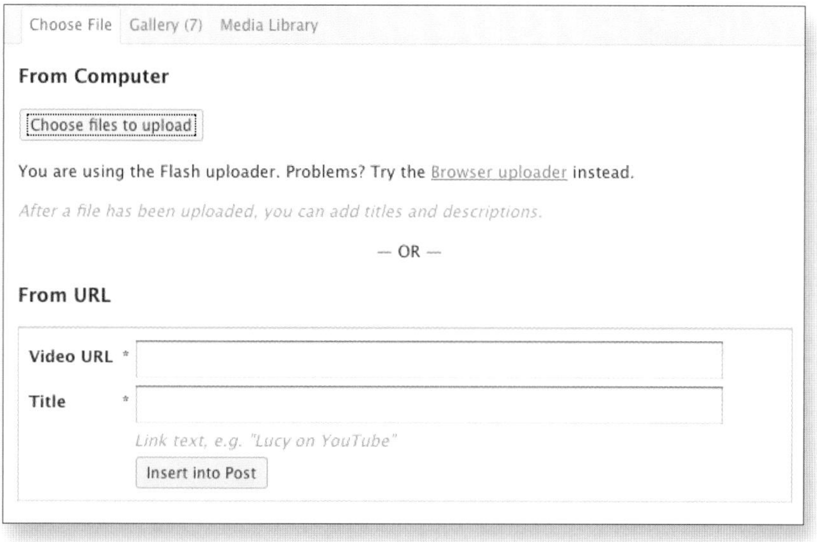

From Computer

Choose File   Gallery (7)   Media Library

Choose files to upload

You are using the Flash uploader. Problems? Try the Browser uploader instead.

After a file has been uploaded, you can add titles and descriptions.

— OR —

From URL

Video URL *

Title   *

Link text, e.g. "Lucy on YouTube"

Insert into Post

Figure 6.27 Uploading a video is just as easy as uploading an image.

The uploader comes in two flavors: Flash and browser (refer to "Adding images" earlier in this chapter). I recommend using the Flash uploader because it displays a progress bar; most of these "other" media types are larger than image files.

 note WordPress respects the parameters for PHP (the language that WordPress itself is written in) in the php.ini file. This file defines several settings for PHP, one of which is maximum upload file size. Depending on how PHP is set up, you may have a maximum file size for uploading. Check with your hosting company.

Using Media Library

I haven't yet talked about one other tab of the media uploader: Media Library (**Figure 6.28**). Media Library is a feature that tracks all the files you've uploaded, no matter what posts you did the uploading from. Because all those files are listed in this tab, you can reinsert media that you've already uploaded without having to upload it again, saving valuable disk space.

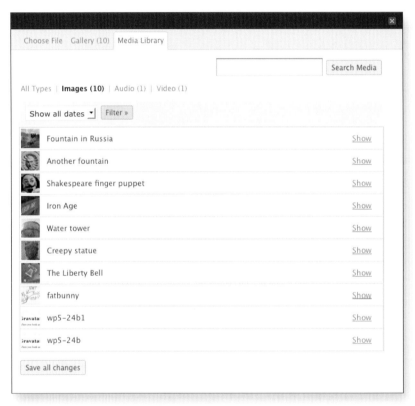

Figure 6.28 Media Library shows all the media that you've uploaded to your blog.

Media Library organizes files by type, so you can look at everything you've uploaded or just images, audio, or video files.

After you've been blogging for a while, you'll probably gather quite a few files in each category, so looking at files by category will be less useful. For that reason, you can also filter Media Library's display by date. Make a choice from the Show All Dates drop-down menu to display only media that you uploaded during a particular month of a particular year (**Figure 6.29**)

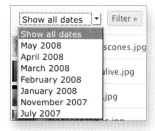

Figure 6.29 You can filter Media Library further: by time.

Limiting results by date has its place. But what if, after applying that filter, you still can't find what you're looking for? You can search your files as well. Enter a keyword in the search text box at the top of the Media Library tab and then click the Search Media button; Media Library returns any and all matches (**Figure 6.30**).

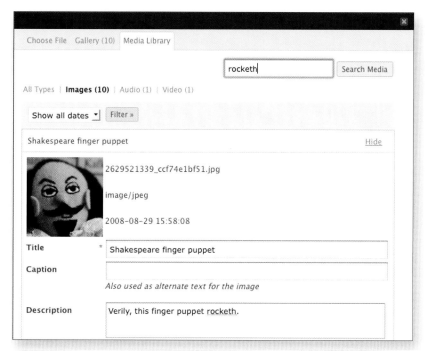

Figure 6.30 Searching Media Library returns any piece of media that matches the search term.

No matter how you filter Media Library's contents, you always see the title of the file and a Show link. Clicking the Show link displays the selected file's settings and allows you to insert that file into the post you're writing.

If you're looking for a particular piece of media that you've uploaded to your blog, choose Manage > Media Library. Choosing this command gives you a slightly different view of Media Library's contents: a list of all the posts in which the item appears (**Figure 6.31**). Another difference: When you click the file's name to open its edit page, you don't get as many options. All you can change are the file's title, caption, and description.

Figure 6.31 Media Library as it appears when you choose Manage > Media Library.

Creating Tags and Categories

One of the first things any new blogger asks me is "How did you get in my house?", quickly followed by "What's the difference between tags and categories?" WordPress supports both of them, right there in the Post panel. The confusion lies in the fact that tags and categories are similar in concept but have key differences.

Tags

Tags are very hip nowadays. If you've used any so-called Web 2.0 site, chances are that you've been asked to tag something (photos, videos, you name it). *Tags* are words or phrases that explain or further describe an object.

If you're writing a post for a book about blogging, for example, you could use some of these words as tags.

- blogging

- lame example

- book

A tag can be any word or phrase you can think of. Tags don't need to be set by the blog's administrator, so any user who can post to the blog can add as many tags as she wants.

Using tags in WordPress

In this section, I give you a look at how tagging works in WordPress.

Figure 6.32 shows the expanded Tags section in the Post panel. (Just click the white down arrow to expand any collapsed options in the panel.) This post doesn't have any tags yet.

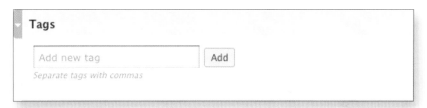

Figure 6.32 The tag entry form. If you want to enter more than one tag, just separate the tags with commas.

If you want to use the word *book* as a tag, all you have to do is type **book** in the text box and then click the Add button. WordPress adds **book** to the new Tags Used on This Post section (**Figure 6.33**).

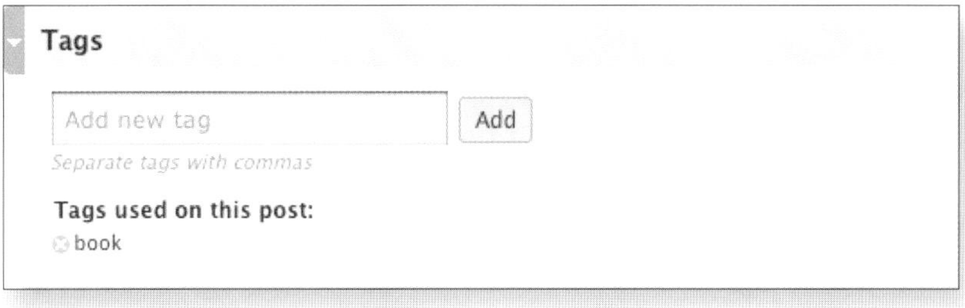

Figure 6.33 The tag **book** has been added.

This post needs a few more tags, so type the following entry in the text box:

screenshot, tagging, fake latin, awesome doodle, this is a long
tag to the post

Click the Add button, and you'll see all these tags added (**Figure 6.34**).

Figure 6.34 New tags.

That silly picture of a bunny that I inserted into the post isn't an awesome doodle, so the awesome doodle tag really doesn't belong. To delete this tag (or any other) from the post, simply click the X next to it.

Keeping tags consistent

One of the biggest problems with tags is also, oddly enough, their greatest strength: They aren't organized in any way. There's no hierarchy of tags, so anyone can use any old phrase as a tag. Inconsistencies pop up when you have more than one person tagging posts. (Should a post about videogames be tagged video games, videogames, or video-games, for example?) WordPress keeps track of all the tags that have been used in a post and does some smart suggesting to keep your tags consistent.

As you type a tag, WordPress is checking what you're typing against its list of existing tags and categories. If it finds any matches, it displays those existing tags (**Figure 6.35**).

Figure 6.35 Autocompletion of tags helps you keep track of your tags.

You can either continue typing to add a tag that's not in the list or click an item in the list and have WordPress fill in the rest for you. Neat, huh? This feature ensures that tags have at least a little consistency.

Categories

Categories have been around for as long as people have been sorting things into groups. If you were to categorize food, you organize it in categories like fruit, vegetables, meat, and dairy. Categories—unlike their flighty siblings, tags—are very well defined. You can think of categories as a hierarchy into which you plug the various bits of content in your blog. (Posts, pages, and links can all have categories.)

Here, you can create new categories or pick categories from a list. The example shown in **Figure 6.36** shows a few existing categories in a blog.

Figure 6.36 Categories are related to tags but are more hierarchical.

 note Uncategorized is a default category that ships with WordPress; it's applied to all posts unless you change that behavior by choosing Setting > Writing > Default Post Category.

Adding categories

You can add new categories right from the Post panel. Just follow these steps:

1. Click the Add New Category link.

    WordPress displays a text box and a drop-down menu below the link.

Only users who have Administrator or Editor privileges see this link. For more information on user roles, see Chapter 3.

2. Type a new category name in the text box.

3. To assign the new category to a parent category (essentially making it a subcategory of the parent category), choose the parent from the drop-down menu.

   The example shown in **Figure 6.37** adds a new category called Tutorials as a subcategory of WordPress. As you see in **Figure 6.38**, the subcategory is listed below the parent category.

Figure 6.37 A category can be assigned to a parent category. In this example, Tutorials is a subcategory of WordPress.

Figure 6.38 A subcategory is listed below its parent category.

Selecting Tutorials as the category for this post doesn't actually add the parent category (WordPress), as you might expect. WordPress knows that any posts categorized as Tutorial are also related to the WordPress category, however. When you visit the parent category's permalink, WordPress also displays all posts categorized in its subcategories. In this example, a user who visits www.wordpressforall/category/wordpress sees all the posts categorized in both the WordPress and Tutorials categories.

You don't have to apply both parent categories and subcategories to a post, but feel free to do so if that makes you happy. You can apply as many categories to a post as you have categories in your blog. Click the check box next to each category that you want the post to be in (**Figure 6.39**). If you click the wrong one, worry not; click again, and that post won't go into that category.

Figure 6.39 You can add as many categories as you like.

Keeping track of categories

Because categories need to exist before they can be applied to a post, it stands to reason that before long, you'll accumulate many categories. Having lots of categories can be a bit overwhelming, but that's why WordPress provides the Most Used link in the Categories section, which opens the Most Used tab (**Figure 6.40**). This tab lists the categories you use most often—a feature that comes in very handy when you have more than ten categories.

Figure 6.40 The Most Used tab gives you easy access to the categories that you use time and time again.

Setting Advanced Posting Options

Take a deep breath. I've covered the basic parts of a WordPress post, and now I'm going to delve into the advanced options.

Right below the Categories section of the Post panel are the Advanced Options settings. The great thing about advanced options is that you need to fiddle with them only if you're really interested in them. At least 99 percent of the time, the default values will serve your needs.

Excerpt

Sometimes you don't want to display the full text of your post. If you choose to show summaries in your feed (see Chapter 5 for feed settings), only a small part of your post is displayed. Likewise, a snippet of your post is displayed in search results and archive pages, depending on your theme. WordPress automatically creates these snippets, called *teasers,* by using the first 55 characters of your post.

The Excerpt panel (**Figure 6.41**) gives you more control of what WordPress displays in these circumstances. You can create a summary of a long post, which will likely be more useful to your readers than the first 55 words. You can set this option on a per-post basis.

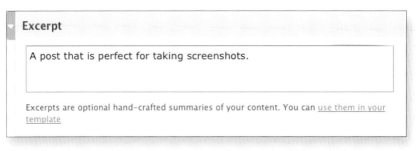

Figure 6.41 An excerpt is a custom summary of your post, which some themes use.

Trackbacks

In the Trackbacks section (**Figure 6.42**), enter the URL of any posts that you want to ping. (See Chapter 6 for more information on trackbacks.) If you want to track back to more than one post, separate the URLs you type in this text box with spaces.

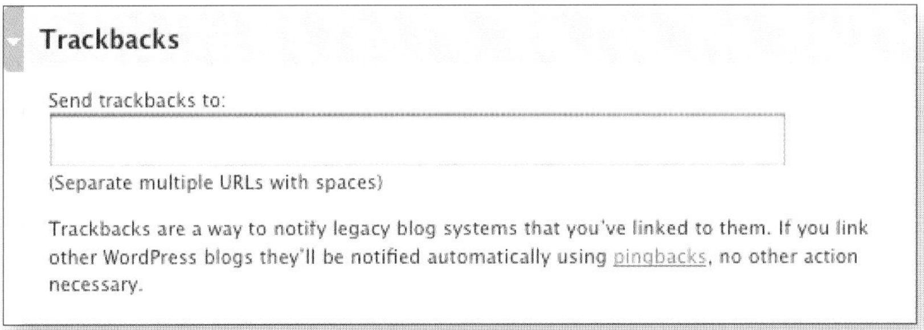

Trackbacks

Send trackbacks to:

(Separate multiple URLs with spaces)

Trackbacks are a way to notify legacy blog systems that you've linked to them. If you link other WordPress blogs they'll be notified automatically using pingbacks, no other action necessary.

Figure 6.42 Enter trackback URLs in the Send Trackbacks To text box.

Custom Fields

The Custom Fields section (**Figure 6.43**) is the most advanced section of advanced options—and the most powerful. WordPress uses several predefined fields to hold data about your posts: title, body, and the like. The Custom Fields section allows you to add your own metadata to posts, which is just a fancy way of saying that you can add arbitrary data that either describes or augments your post using Custom Fields. In the Key text box, you enter a name for the custom field; in the Value text box, enter the content of that field. Then click the Add Custom Field button to complete the process.

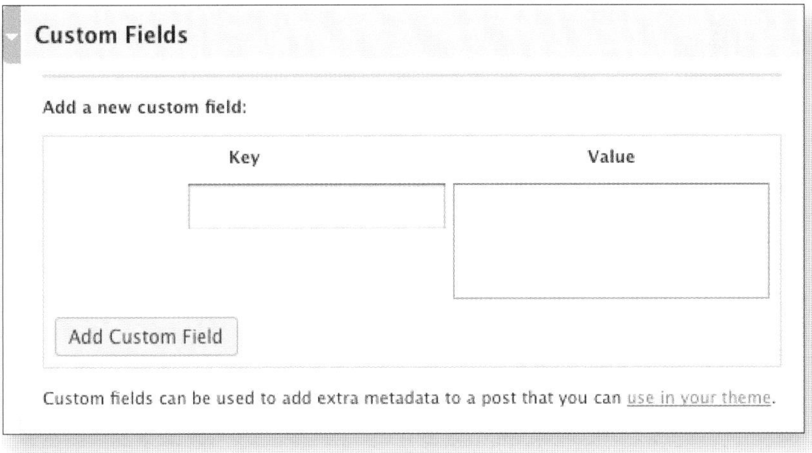

Custom Fields

Add a new custom field:

Key

Value

Add Custom Field

Custom fields can be used to add extra metadata to a post that you can use in your theme.

Figure 6.43 Adding your own metadata to a post is simple business, thanks to Custom Fields.

Comments & Pings

A blog is akin to a discussion. You put your thoughts out into the world, and random people can share their opinions with you by leaving comments or by using trackbacks to send your post a ping. The Comments & Pings section (**Figure 6.44**) allows you to turn pings and comments on or off on a per-post basis. These settings override the global comment/ping settings, which you access by choosing Settings > Discussion.

Figure 6.44 Comments and pings can be enabled or disabled on a per-post basis.

Password Protect This Post

Blogs generally are open to the public. Anyone can read any or all of your posts. If you want to limit access to a post's content, however, you can set a password on that post by typing it in the Password Protect This Post section. Anyone who knows the password (which you have to share with them) can read the post by entering the password. WordPress displays *Protected:* before the post's title so that people know that the post's contents are password protected (**Figure 6.45**).

Figure 6.45 A password-protected post.

 note The password protection you set here extends to your blog's feed. Subscribers to the feed will know that you have a password-protected post, but they won't be privy to its contents without the password.

Post Author

Users with Administrator and Editor privileges can change a post's author by making a new choice from the Post Author drop-down menu (**Figure 6.46**), which lists all the users of your blog in alphabetical order.

Figure 6.46 Authorship of a post can be assigned to any user of the blog.

Post Revisions

As you're typing away in your post, crafting a literary gem, WordPress is hard at work making sure that you'll never lose a single character of that brilliance. In addition to ensuring that none of your work is lost (or at least, not much of it) if your browser quits, this autosave feature enables WordPress to track revisions of your post. Want your post to look like it did an hour ago? As long as WordPress has a saved version from an hour ago, you can return to the past by clicking a link in the Post Revisions section (**Figure 6.47**). WordPress automatically saves all the revisions forever. At the moment, WordPress doesn't have an interface that allows you to delete revisions or to set how long it holds on to them.

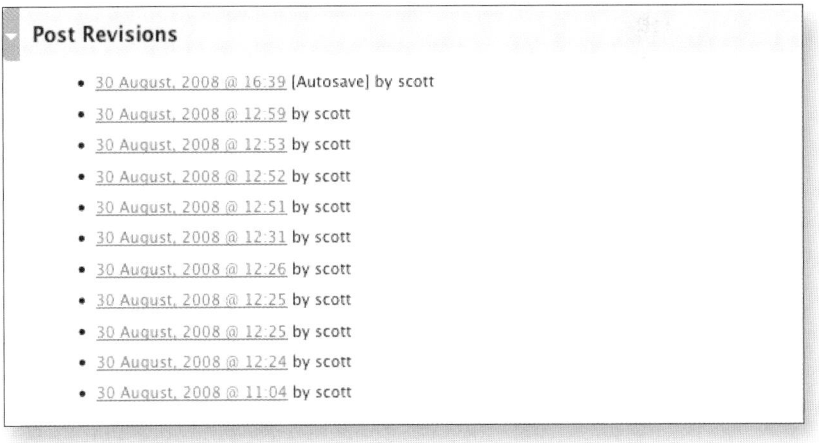

Post Revisions

- 30 August, 2008 @ 16:39 [Autosave] by scott
- 30 August, 2008 @ 12:59 by scott
- 30 August, 2008 @ 12:53 by scott
- 30 August, 2008 @ 12:52 by scott
- 30 August, 2008 @ 12:51 by scott
- 30 August, 2008 @ 12:31 by scott
- 30 August, 2008 @ 12:26 by scott
- 30 August, 2008 @ 12:25 by scott
- 30 August, 2008 @ 12:25 by scott
- 30 August, 2008 @ 12:24 by scott
- 30 August, 2008 @ 11:04 by scott

Figure 6.47 WordPress tracks the changes made in posts.

When you click a link for one of your revisions, WordPress displays the post exactly as it appeared at that time. If what you're seeing isn't what you want, just click another Post Revisions link.

When you're confident that you want to revert to a previous revision, just click the Restore radio button next to the revision you want (**Figure 6.48**). If you decide that you don't want to restore any previous version, just click the post's title at the top of the page; WordPress returns to your post, which is as you left it.

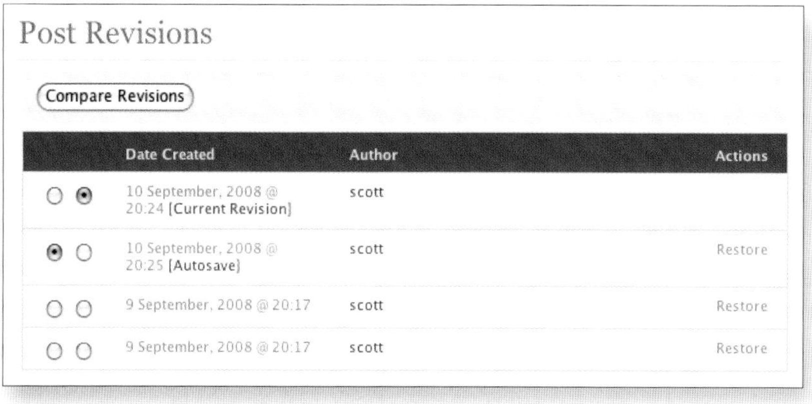

Figure 6.48 Click Restore to revert to an older revision.

7

Publishing Your Post (Finally!)

Your post is ready, and the Publish Status section of the Post panel looks like **Figure 7.1** (on the next page). You set everything the way you want it (see Chapter 5), assigned categories and tags (see Chapter 6), and ran a spell check. The only thing left is to publish your post, right?

Perhaps not. You may still want to do a few things before you click the Publish button to make your post live. Also, even after your post is live on your blog, you may want to go back into it and edit the contents, change tags or categories, or even delete it. This chapter covers all the details of posting that aren't specifically content related.

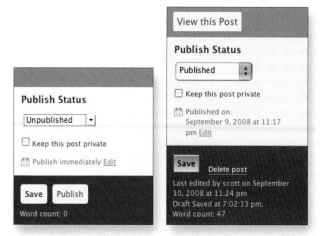

Figure 7.1 Two versions of the Publish Status section. The one on the left is for a post that has yet to be saved or published; the one on the right provides options for a published/saved post.

Previewing a Post

If you click the Save button in the Publish Status section, a Preview This Post button appears atop the other publishing options on the right side of the screen. Click this button to see what your post will look like on your blog. The preview looks exactly as your post will look when you publish it, revealing any formatting problems that your theme may cause (which I discuss further in chapters 11 and 12).

Setting Publishing Status

After you preview your post, you're ready to set its publishing status. To do this, you choose an option from the drop-down menu in the Publish Status section (**Figure 7.2**).

Figure 7.2 The Publish Status drop-down menu.

Keeping a Post Private

When you publish a post, it's accessible on the Web via its perma-link and also appears on the front page of your blog (unless you change your index-page options, which I talk about in Chapter 12). Suppose, however, that you have a post that you want only a certain segment of your audience to read. In the Publish Status section, simply check the Keep This Post Private check box. When you enable this option, your post is published, but not to your blog's front page. Then you can share the link with only the people you want to read the post.

Don't worry that someone else will stumble upon the post by looking at your site's directories. WordPress doesn't create static files for your posts; it generates each post dynamically. If visitors don't have the link to a post, and if the post isn't published on your blog's main page, they can't find it.

You have three choices:

- **Unpublished.** This setting is the default for a newly created post, known as a *draft*. If you save a post as unpublished, the draft isn't posted to your blog but saved for later editing.

- **Published.** Choose this option to publish the post to your blog immediately.

- **Pending Review.** When a post is set to Pending Review, users with Administrator or Editor privileges know to take a look at the post and publish it by looking at the list of pending posts (which I cover in more detail in a moment).

Posting to Your Blog

When you're finally ready to make a post live on your blog, click the Publish button in the Publish Status section. When you do, a few things happen:

1. The post is saved.

2. The Publish Status drop-down menu is set to Published.

3. The post is posted to your blog.

Scheduling posts

Sometimes, however, you want to write a blog post before an event and have the post publish itself at a certain time. To do this, click the Edit link in the Publish Status section, right after the words *Publish immediately*. WordPress displays the scheduling controls shown in **Figure 7.3**. You can enter a date and time for your post to go live (and backdate posts, too). Be sure to enter the time in 24-hour format, as shown in the figure, because WordPress uses a 24-hour clock.

Figure 7.3 Scheduling a post.

 tip Check the time-zone setting on your server. If the time zone isn't set correctly, your posts may not go live at the times you've scheduled.

Viewing postpublishing options

The dark gray area at the bottom of the Publish Status section contains some items of note (**Figure 7.4**). The Save button saves your post. If you go back and edit an older post, all you have to do is click Save to publish your changes. Clicking the Publish button in a newly created post, of course, publishes the post. Finally, if you want to get rid of the post entirely, click the Delete Post link.

Figure 7.4 Even more publishing options.

 When you hover your mouse pointer over the Delete Post link, the link turns red to warn you that there's no turning back. After you click the link, the post and all its saved revisions are gone.

Below the save options is some information about the post itself: who last edited the post and when, when the draft was saved, and how many words are in the post.

Using the Press This Shortcut

At the bottom of the rightmost column of the Post panel is a section called Shortcuts. It's unclear to me why this section is called Shortcuts instead of Shortcut, because only one shortcut is listed, but such are the mysteries of life. The Press This link (the sole shortcut)—short for *WordPress this*—is actually a JavaScript bookmarklet. *Bookmarklets* are simple additions to your browser that don't actually bookmark Web sites; instead, they perform a task (or series of tasks) based on what Web site you're viewing. Drag the Press This bookmarklet into your browser's bookmarks bar, and you can post to your blog simply by clicking the link (**Figure 7.5** on the next page).

Figure 7.5 The Press This bookmarklet installed in Mozilla Firefox.

The Press This bookmarklet does a clever thing: It inserts the title and link of the page you're viewing into a post. Then you can simply post the link or add some commentary.

Press This also makes it very easy to post links, text, and video that you find while surfing the Net.

 note   **Remember to properly attribute anything that you use from another source (typically by linking back to the source).**

When you click Press This while viewing a Web page, WordPress displays the Press This dialog box, which has four tabs representing the feature's four modes: Text, Photo, Quote, and Video. I discuss all four tabs in the following sections.

Press This: Text

Text mode is your best choice when you want to write a long post about the page that struck your fancy. Click Press This while you're looking at a Web site to open the Press This dialog box, which opens by default to the Text tab (**Figure 7.6**). (If you aren't logged in to your blog, you have to log in first; then you're taken to the Text tab.) A link to the page you're viewing is entered in the Post text box automatically, and the Title text box is set to the title of the Web page.

The Text tab offers a subset of the features you find in the regular WordPress posting interface. This mini posting form uses the Visual Editor, but your formatting options are fairly limited. Still, you can bold-face, italicize, and underline text; you can create block quotes, numbered lists, and bulleted lists; and you can insert links.

Finally, the right side of the tab provides controls for adding tags and categories. (For details on those features, flip back to Chapter 6.)

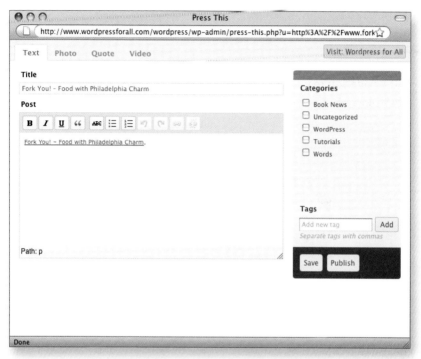

Figure 7.6 WordPress starts you off in Text mode by entering a suggested title and the URL of the post you're viewing.

Press This: Photo

The Photo tab (**Figure 7.7**) is even smarter than the Text tab: It collects all the images on a page and displays them for you. Then you can add as many of them as you like to your post simply by dragging and dropping.

 note Keep in mind that any images you insert in this fashion are hotlinked, so you don't want to abuse this feature.

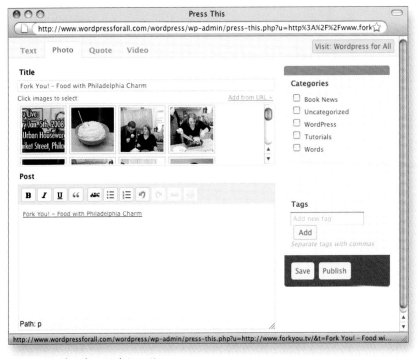

Figure 7.7 The Photo tab in action.

You can't access your Media Library or upload media from this tab, but you can add an image from a URL the same way that you do in the full posting interface. I cover all the details in Chapter 6.

Press This: Quote

The Quote tab is a great tool if you like to quote big chunks of text from other sites. To use it, select the text you want to quote and click the Press This link in your browser's bookmarks bar. WordPress displays the Press This dialog box, open to the Quote tab; the selected text appears in the Quote text box, along with a link back to the source (**Figure 7.8**).

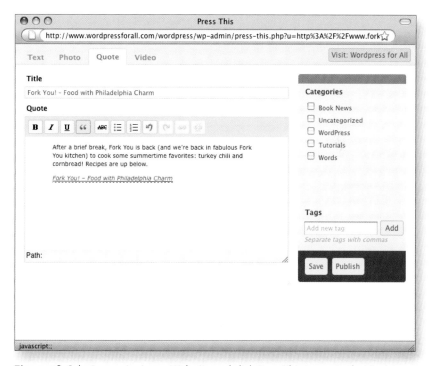

Figure 7.8 Select some text on a Web site and click Press This to quote that text in your post.

Press This: Video

Suppose that you're watching a video on the Web and want to post it on your blog. All you have to do is click the Press This link in your browser's bookmarks bar. The bookmarklet gets the code required to embed the video in your blog and pops it into a post in the Video tab (**Figure 7.9**).

Figure 7.9 The Video tab, displaying embedding code for a video.

This feature doesn't work for every video-sharing site but does work for most of the big ones, including YouTube and Vimeo.

Managing Posts

Directly above the Shortcuts section of the Post panel is a list of links with the header Related Links. These links provide you access to several management pages (which you can also get to by clicking the big Manage tab in the navigation bar of the administrative interface, directly below your blog's title). The first two links involve comments, which I talk about in Chapter 10, so I'll skip those.

Viewing and filtering posts

Clicking the Manage All Posts link takes you to the Manage Posts panel of WordPress (**Figure 7.10**). By default, this panel shows you all the posts that are on your blog, as well as their publishing status.

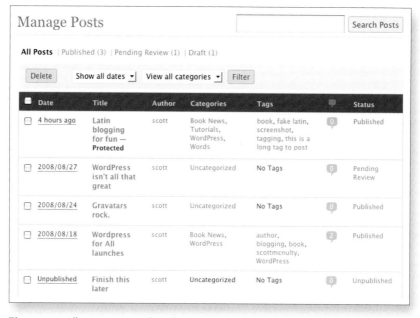

Figure 7.10 All your posts are listed in this panel.

You can filter the posts displayed in the Manage Posts panel in several ways: by publishing status, date, category, by post attributes. I discuss these methods in the following sections.

Filtering by status, date, and category

You can display your posts by publishing status by clicking the various links shown at the top of **Figure 7.11**. The number next to each link shows you how many posts have that particular publishing status, and clicking the link shows you only those posts with that publishing status.

Figure 7.11 The filter options of the Manage Posts panel.

You can also filter posts based on date (much like images in Media Library) or by category. To filter by category, make a choice from the category drop-down menu (**Figure 7.12**). The subcategories appear below their parent categories in the Manage Posts panel.

Figure 7.12 Filtering by category.

Filtering by attributes

The Manage Post panel has seven columns, as you see in Figure 7.10 earlier in this chapter: Date, Title, Author, Category, Tags, Comments, and Status. With the exception of the Date column, all the values in those columns are clickable links. When you click the link in each column, the results are filtered thusly:

- **Title.** Clicking the title takes you to the edit panel for that post.

- **Author.** Shows only the posts penned by that person.

- **Category.** Shows all the posts in that category.

- **Tags.** Shows all the posts featuring that tag.

- **Comments.** The number of comments on the post appears in this bubble. Clicking it lists the comments on that post.

- **Status.** Shows posts by publishing status.

Searching for posts

In addition to filtering posts in the Manage Posts panel, you can search for a specific post. Enter a search term in the text box in the top-right corner, and click Search Posts. WordPress looks for your search term in post contents as well as in post titles, tags, and categories.

Deleting posts

You can delete one or more posts in this panel as well. To delete a single post, click the check box next to its name and then click the Delete button.

If you need to delete several posts that are listed together, click the check box of the first post you want to delete and then Shift-click the check box of the last post you want to delete. WordPress checks all the boxes for the posts in between the two you clicked. Then click the Delete button, and away the posts go.

Checking the number of comments

Finally, you can see quickly what posts have garnered comments from your readers. The column of the Manage Posts panel headed by a little speech bubble (refer to Figure 7.10) displays the number of approved comments for each post. When a post's comment bubble is blue, as it is in **Figure 7.13**, comments on that post are waiting to be approved. Click the bubble to go to the comment-management interface (which I cover in Chapter 10).

Figure 7.13 The number of comments that a post has received.

Managing Categories

Chapter 6 shows you how to add categories and tags to your blog while you're writing a post. But what if you want to create a bunch of categories without having to post something or to delete some tags that you created accidentally? That's where the Manage Categories and Manage Tags panels come in. I discuss the categories panel in this section and cover the tags panel in the next.

Viewing categories

Notice the Manage link in the navigation bar below your blog's title in the WordPress administration interface. Clicking this link is your gateway to managing your blog. Below the management panel are links to various kinds of blog content. Click the Categories link to manage your blog's categories without having to write a post.

Much like the Manage Posts panel (which I cover in the preceding section), the Manage Categories panel lays out categories in a table (**Figure 7.14**). You can search the categories, if you have many, or just eyeball them to find the one you want to delete or edit.

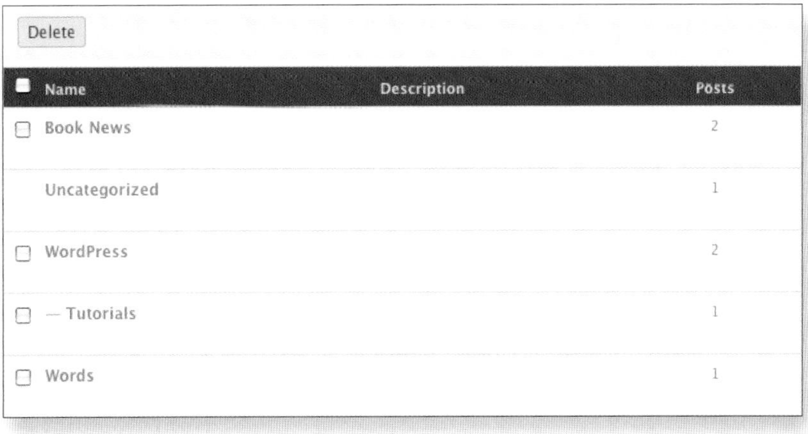

Name	Description	Posts
☐ Book News		2
Uncategorized		1
☐ WordPress		2
☐ — Tutorials		1
☐ Words		1

Figure 7.14 This table gives you some at-a-glance information, including how many posts each category contains.

The three columns are fairly straightforward:

- **Name** lists the name of the category. (Subcategories are listed below their parents.)

- **Description** provides an optional description of the category (see the next section).

- **Posts** shows you how many posts are in that category. Clicking a number in this column takes you to the Manage Posts page, which displays the posts filtered by category (refer to "Filtering by status, date, and category" earlier in this chapter).

Editing categories

Click the name of a category listed in the Manage Categories panel to edit it. WordPress opens the Edit Category dialog box (**Figure 7.15**).

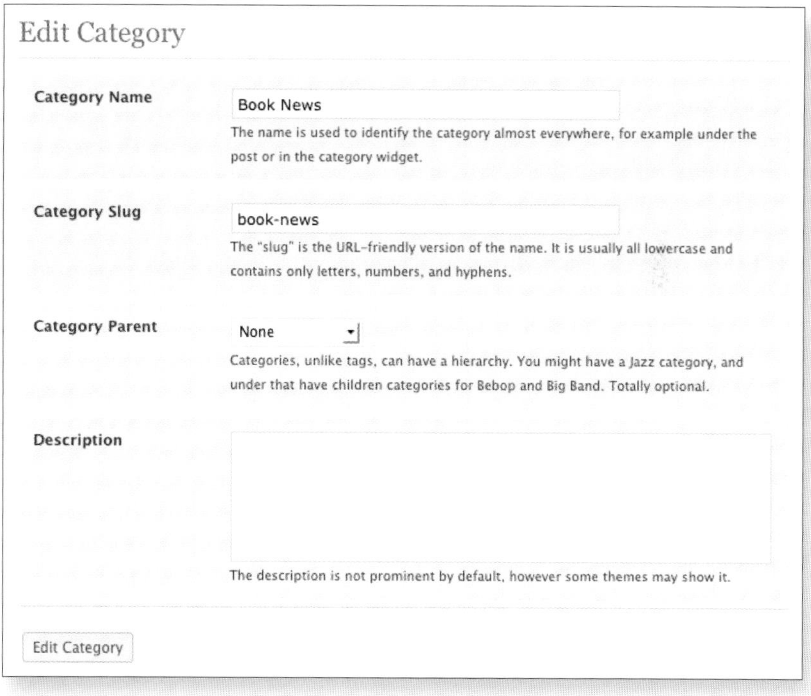

Edit Category

Category Name	Book News
	The name is used to identify the category almost everywhere, for example under the post or in the category widget.
Category Slug	book-news
	The "slug" is the URL-friendly version of the name. It is usually all lowercase and contains only letters, numbers, and hyphens.
Category Parent	None
	Categories, unlike tags, can have a hierarchy. You might have a Jazz category, and under that have children categories for Bebop and Big Band. Totally optional.
Description	
	The description is not prominent by default, however some themes may show it.

Edit Category

Figure 7.15 Edit WordPress categories in this dialog box.

You can set the following options:

- **Category Name.** This setting is the name that's displayed in your posts, and it's what you see in the various category lists in the WordPress administrator interface. Make sure that this name is meaningful.

- **Category Slug.** Although this name may sound like an insult, it isn't. The *slug* is the last part of the category permalink (refer to Chapter 6). Make sure that you type the slug using only lowercase letters, numbers, and hyphens.

 You can change the name of an existing category, but avoid changing the category's slug. If you rename the slug, you'll break all the links that point to the old slug-based permalinks. (Breaking links is bad.)

- **Category Parent.** You can assign any category a parent category, though this setting is optional. You can also change a subcategory's parent category. Further, you can assign a subcategory as another category's parent (which would make it a subsubcategory, I suppose), though that's as deep as subcategorization can go.

- **Description.** Describe your category in this text box, if you want. Most themes don't display this information, however, so it's optional (though perhaps most themes don't display the information because it's optional, which in turn is why it's optional—whoa!).

When you finish, click the Edit Category button to save your changes.

Adding categories

Clicking the Add Category link at the top of the Manage Categories panel takes you to the Add Category form (**Figure 7.16**). The options are the same as those in the Edit Category dialog box (which I cover in the preceding section). Add the information that you want and click the Add Category button, and you're good to go.

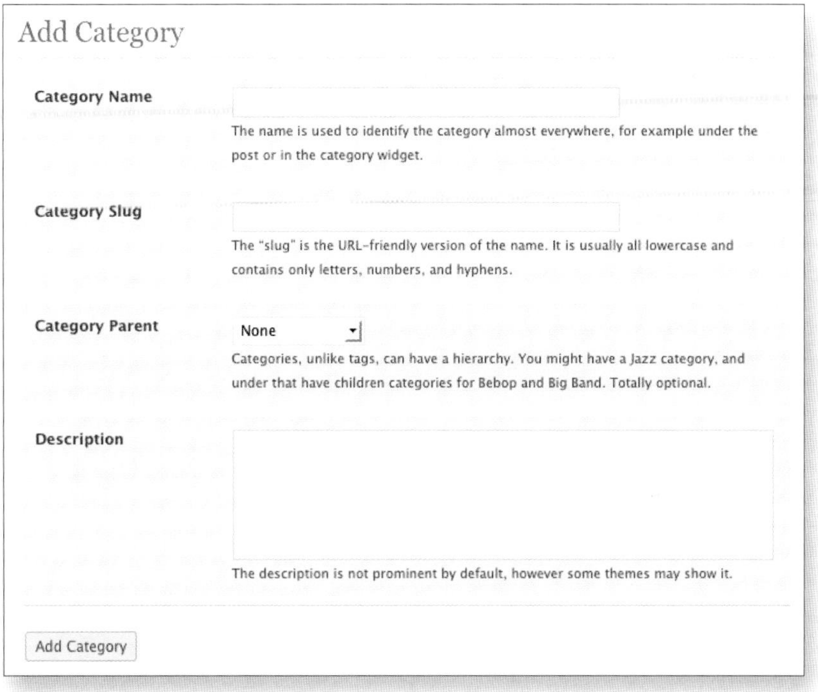

Add Category

Category Name	
	The name is used to identify the category almost everywhere, for example under the post or in the category widget.
Category Slug	
	The "slug" is the URL-friendly version of the name. It is usually all lowercase and contains only letters, numbers, and hyphens.
Category Parent	None
	Categories, unlike tags, can have a hierarchy. You might have a Jazz category, and under that have children categories for Bebop and Big Band. Totally optional.
Description	
	The description is not prominent by default, however some themes may show it.

Add Category

Figure 7.16 The Add Category form.

> **tip** WordPress wants to help you help yourself. If you enter a slug or category name that already exists, WordPress throws an error and highlights the duplicate information in red (*Figure 7.17*).

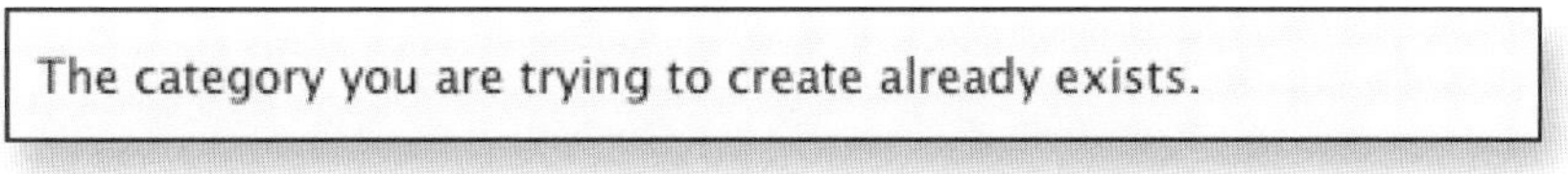

The category you are trying to create already exists.

Figure 7.17 A warning that you tried to create a duplicate category.

Deleting categories

Deleting categories is just like deleting posts (refer to the section of the same name earlier in this chapter). Click the check box next to the category you want to delete (or Shift-click to select contiguous categories); then click the Delete button. The category is removed from all the posts to which it was applied.

If any posts were categorized with only the deleted category, WordPress automatically reassigns those posts to the default Uncategorized category.

Managing Tags

Not surprisingly, tag management is similar to category management. Your tags are displayed in a list in the Manage Tags panel, just as categories are displayed in the Manage Categories panel. The Posts column shows you how many posts use the tag in question (**Figure 7.18**). Clicking a number in that column takes you to the Manage Posts panel, which is filtered by that tag.

Name	Posts
author	1
blogging	1
book	2

Figure 7.18 Managing tags involves the familiar tabular display.

You can also use the panel's search controls to search for a specific tag.

Editing tags

Clicking a tag's name in the Name column opens the Edit Tag dialog box (**Figure 7.19**).

Tags are simpler than categories, a fact that's reflected in the settings you can edit (all two of them):

- **Tag Name.** This name is the one that shows up on your blog, so it can contain any character that you can type.

- **Tag Slug.** Just like the category slug (refer to "Editing categories" earlier in this chapter), the tag slug is part of your tag's permalink; it should contain only lowercase letters, numbers, and hyphens.

note   Don't change tag slugs later; if you do, you'll break permalinks left and right.

Edit Tag

Tag name

about

The name is how the tag appears on your site.

Tag slug

about

The "slug" is the URL–friendly version of the name. It is usually all lowercase and contains only letters, numbers, and hyphens.

Edit Tag

Figure 7.19 The Edit Tag dialog box.

Adding tags

Clicking Add Tags at the top of the Manage Tags panel takes you to the Add Tag form. Enter a name and a slug, and click the Add Tag button. Your tag is available for use in your blog.

Converting Tags and Categories

I hope that I've made it clear that although on the surface, tags and categories seem to do the same things, they have some differences. What happens if you want to convert one or all of your categories to tags, or if you decide that you hate tags and that categories are the way to go? Are you stuck? Nope. WordPress has a great converter that does the following jobs:

- Changes your tags to categories and applies the new categories to the posts that were previously tagged

- Changes your categories to tags and tags the formerly categorized posts with your new hotness (the new tags, not the actual words *new hotness*)

continues on next page

Converting Tags and Categories *continued*

Changing a category to a tag

To change a category to a tag, follow these steps:

1. Go to www.*yourWordPressURL*.com/wp-admin/admin.php?import=
    wp-cat2tag, or choose Manage > Import > Categories and Tags Converter.

 You can find out what your WordPress URL is by choosing Settings > General.

2. Check the category you want to change.

    An asterisk next to a category's name (**Figure 7.20**) means that a tag with
    that same name exists. In this case, the category will be deleted, and the
    posts that were in that category will get the existing tag applied to them.

Figure 7.20 A category that shares a name with an existing tag.

3. Click the Convert Categories to Tags button.

    WordPress does the rest.

The duration of the process depends on the number of posts in the category that's being converted to a tag. (The more posts in the category, the
longer the conversion takes.) When the conversion is complete,
WordPress informs you that the process was successful.

Changing a tag to a category

The following URL takes you directly to the Tags to Categories converter:

www.*yourWordPressURL*.com/wp-admin/admin.php?import=
wp-cat2tag&step=3

The process is the same as changing a tag to a category, only this time,
you're selecting a tag to change instead of a category.

8

Working with Pages

When you create a page (either by clicking the Write a New Page button in the Dashboard or by clicking the Write link in the navigation bar below your blog's title and then clicking Page), you'll be struck by how similar the Page panel is to the Post panel.

Pages have the same basic structure as posts, consisting of a title and a body section. They list the authors of posts and can contain custom fields. They also can be password protected. The similarities end there, however.

Think of a page as a nonchronological post. Posts are moments in time; they flow across your blog like water across a riverbed. Pages aren't tied to any particular time or date; they contain information that, though not necessarily static, isn't as malleable.

Although a page's content may be static, the page itself isn't. Like the rest of WordPress content, pages are generated dynamically via templates, which I discuss in this chapter. Pages always display the most-up-to-date information because they're generated dynamically.

Working with Page Settings

Most of the settings that are available for pages in WordPress are the same as those for posts. Three settings are page-specific: Page Parent, Page Template, and Page Order. These settings are what make pages something more than posts.

Page Parent

Just as you can turn a category into a subcategory by assigning a parent category to it (see Chapter 6), you can create a subpage by assigning a parent to that page. Subpages, which you can nest as deep as you like, are displayed below their parent pages. This feature is an easy way to give your pages some organization and make them easier to navigate.

Assigning a Page Parent is easy. Each page starts as a main page, meaning that it has no parent. Clicking the Page Parent drop-down menu (**Figure 8.1**) shows you a list of all your published pages—both main pages and any subpages (indented below their parent pages). Choose a page to be the parent of the page you're currently editing, and you're done—though the changes won't be saved until you save or publish the page.

Figure 8.1 The Page Parent setting makes creating hierarchical page groups easy.

Page Template

Much of a page's awesomeness comes from its Page Template setting (**Figure 8.2**) Different themes have different default page templates, so check your theme's documentation for that information.

Figure 8.2 You can set the template your page uses by choosing it from the drop-down menu.

Understanding templates

First, I need to explain what templates are and how they relate to your blog. When you come right down to it, WordPress is just a bunch of files. *Templates* are special types of files that control the way information is rendered on your blog. Templates define how your content behaves, displaying it in a consistent manner.

 Not all themes include template files. If you don't see the Page Template option in the Page panel, no templates are available for your theme. You can add templates yourself, which I cover later in this chapter.

Page templates apply this concept to content that is common across blogs. Different themes (see chapters 11 and 12) include different templates for pages. Later in this chapter, I show you how to create your own custom template.

Using the default WordPress templates

The default WordPress theme comes with two page templates:

- **Archives.** The Archives template is used in conjunction with special tags to create an archive of older posts. When this template is applied to a page, WordPress ignores anything you type in the body of the page. Instead, the page displays only two lists: your blog posts by month and posts by category. Most blogs include an archive so that your readers can easily browse your backlog of posts. This template makes it very easy to create an archive for your blog (**Figure 8.3**).

Figure 8.3 An example of a page using the Archive template.

- **Links.** Links is a simple template that displays all your links grouped by category (**Figure 8.4**). This template is a great one to use if you want to maintain a page of all the links you're keeping track of in your blog. You can also use this template to create a *blogroll* (a list of links to blogs that your read). Chapter 9 is all about links and what you can do with them.

Figure 8.4 An example of a page using the Links template.

If you're using a theme other than the WordPress default theme for your blog, you may have access to different templates—or to none at all. Consult your theme's documentation for a full list. See chapters 11 and 12 for details on themes.

note   Comments and pings are enabled by default when you create a new page, but in some cases a page that has comments enabled provides no way for anyone to leave a comment. In these cases, the template being used doesn't include the code for the comment form. (The default templates fall into this category.)

Page Order

The Page Order setting is a bit of a hack at the moment, but the WordPress developers promise that it will get better. Normally, pages are listed in alphabetical order. If you want your pages to be displayed in a different order (perhaps grouping them by topic), enter a number in the Page Order text box (**Figure 8.5**). The lower the number you enter, the earlier the page will be displayed. (Pages with the same page-order number are sorted alphabetically.)

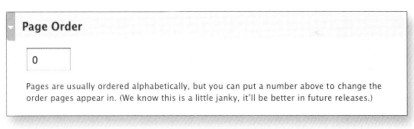

Figure 8.5 Change this setting to display your pages in the order you want.

Suppose that I have three pages in my blog: About, Links, and Colophon. Normally, WordPress displays those pages in alphabetical order, but if I want the Colophon page to be listed first, I just set its Page Order setting to 1. Now Colophon is listed first, and the remaining pages are listed in alphabetical order.

Understanding Page Permalinks

WordPress generates the permalink for a page automatically, based on the page's title, and displays it below the title just as it does for a post (**Figure 8.6**). The key difference between page and post permalinks is the URL structure.

About

Permalink: http://www.wordpressforall.com/about/ Edit

Figure 8.6 The page permalink is displayed below the title.

Here's a link to a post titled "Scott McNulty" on my blog:

www.wordpressforall.com/2008/10/19/scott-mcnulty/

The permalink for the "Scott McNulty" page on my blog, however, looks like this:

www.wordpressforall.com/scott-mcnulty/

The page permalink is just the blog URL and the URL *safe title* of the page: the title with spaces replaced by hyphens and any non-URL-friendly characters removed. You can edit this URL, of course, but page permalinks are a little less flexible than post, tag, or category permalinks.

Post permalinks, which I discuss in Chapter 5, are the most flexible type, because you can create a custom permalink structure that allows you to add extensions to all your links (such as .html). You can set the base for tags and category permalinks (the concept of a base for your permalinks is explained in detail in Chapter 5)—a limited capability, but better than what you can do for pages. Page permalinks are always safe titles.

My "Scott McNulty" permalink is a typical page permalink. The only thing I can change about it is the scott-mcnulty part. I can make the text any word—or combination of words, numbers, and hyphens—but I can't put my pages in a different directory or add extensions to the URL. To get that kind of control of page permalinks, I'd have to use a plug-in. (See Chapter 13 for information on WordPress plug-ins.)

Creating a Page Template

Creating your own page template is straightforward, as the simple example in this section shows. The process gets more complicated when you want the template to do something more useful. Chapter 12, which deals with themes, covers a few of the WordPress tags you can use to turn this template from a proof of concept to something that may be useful for your blog.

Page templates are located in the root of your theme's folder. For this example, you add a template to the default WordPress theme.

To create an example page template, follow these steps:

1. Open your text editor of choice.

   I like TextMate in Mac OS X, but you can use any free text editor that's available for your platform, such as Notepad or TextEdit.

2. Type the following code:

   ```php
   <?php
   /*
   Template Name: Example Template
   */
   ?>
   ```

   This code tells WordPress that the file is a page template. The `Template Name` parameter sets the name of the template, which will be displayed in the Page Template drop-down menu (refer to "Page Template" earlier in this chapter). In this example, you name the template `Example Template` because I have no imagination.

   The rest of the template is code that does something.

3. Enter the rest of the example template, which calls the header and footer of the current theme and displays a message:

   ```php
   <?php get_header(); ?>
   <div>
   Hello, world!
   </div>
   <?php get_footer(); ?>
   ```

4. Save the template as a PHP file.

   Make sure that the file extension is .php; otherwise, the file won't work.

5. Upload the template to the default theme folder, which is located here in your WordPress installation:

   wordpress/wp-content/themes/default/

note *wordpress* **is the directory containing your WordPress installation.**

The template should appear in the Page Template drop-down menu now (**Figure 8.7**). Pretty cool, huh?

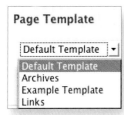

Figure 8.7 The example template displayed with the rest of the page templates.

If you visited a page that actually used this template, though, the template wouldn't serve any useful purpose; it wouldn't even display the `Hello, world!` message in an attractive way. See Chapter 12 for details on transforming this template into a helpful page.

Managing Pages

Managing pages is very similar to managing posts. To open the Manage Pages panel, choose Manage > Pages. The panel's page list displays the date each page was posted, the title, the author, how many comments the page has received, and its publication status (**Figure 8.8**).

	Date	Title	Author	🗨	Status
☐	2008/08/11	About	admin	0	Published
☐	46 mins ago	— Scott McNulty	scott	0	Published

Delete

Figure 8.8 Pages listed in the Manage Pages panel.

At the top of the panel are a few links that filter the page list based on publishing status (**Figure 8.9**). Each link—Published, Pending Review, and Draft—is followed by a number in parentheses that tells you how many pages have that status. If you don't have any pages with a particular status, that link isn't displayed.

Manage Pages

All Pages | Published (2) | Pending Review (1) | Draft (1)

Figure 8.9 Filtering links in the Manage Pages panel.

This panel provides a search feature that searches both body and title content of your pages and returns anything that matches.

If you want to edit a page, click the title, and you'll be taken to the Edit Page dialog box, where you can change the settings or content. You can even apply a new page template, if you like.

Deleting pages is just like deleting a post (see Chapter 7). Click the check box next to the page you want to delete, or Shift-click to select more than one page, and click the Delete button.

9

Handling Links

Posts and pages are like fraternal twins. They have many similar traits, but they aren't exact copies. Links are the red-headed stepchild of the WordPress family. (No offense intended to you actual red-headed stepchildren out there; I'm sure you're fantastic people.) Links bear very little relation to pages and posts. Sure, the interface for managing them is pretty much the same, but links serve a very different purpose from either posts or pages.

In this chapter, I define what links are, show you how to add them to your blog, and go over how to manage your collection of links. I also cover link categories and give you a few ideas on how to use links with your blog.

What the Heck Are Links?

Way back in the early days of blogging (way, way back in the ancient times of 1999), the blogosphere was a small place. A few bloggers linked to one another, and everyone liked this arrangement. Then the introduction of easily installable blogging solutions (like WordPress) opened blogging to a whole new set of people. These people were reading more and more blogs, and they wanted a way to share all the cool blogs they were tracking with their audiences. The blogroll was born, and the Internet has never been the same.

At its core the *blogroll* is a simple concept: a list of links, usually displayed in a *sidebar* (a column of a blog that doesn't contain the blog's main content, usually located on the right side of the page). Fancier blogrolls incorporate pictures and perhaps a link to the blog's feed.

Maintaining blogrolls by hand was laborious, so WordPress added links to the mix. That's why when you check out the prepopulated links by choosing Manage > Links, you find all of them in one category: Blogroll.

Although the links feature of WordPress was designed to display your blogroll, you don't have to limit yourself to that. You can use links to organize and display any sort of link list. Have a bunch of favorite Web comics that you like? Create a Web Comics link category, with a link to each comic. Want to use links for a blogroll, but organize the blogroll by type? Because WordPress doesn't apply the subcategory concept to links, create a category for each type and then assign blogs to the right category (**Figure 9.1**).

Awesome websites
» WordPress For All

Blogroll
» Aarrgghh!!!!
» Apartment 2024
» Asymptomatic
» Blankbaby
» Colin D. Devroe
» ericsmithrocks.com
» Geekadelphia
» Only Partially Insane
» philly
» Squirrels Go Like This

Figure 9.1 Two groups of links in two different categories.

Typically, links are grouped by category when they're displayed on a blog page. You can add as many categories as you want to organize your links (such as Awesome Websites in Figure 9.1; see Chapter 6 for details on adding categories), but you can't delete the Blogroll category.

tip   If you don't want to use the Blogroll category, you can rename it or take all the links out of it. See "Editing and deleting links" later in this chapter for more information.

Configuring Links

Now that you know what links are and why they're an option in WordPress, I'll talk about how to add, edit, and delete them. Much like posts and pages, links are best when they're kept fresh with a little tending and pruning.

Adding links

To add links, first open the Manage Links panel by choosing Manage > Links; then click the Add New link to open the Add Link panel (**Figure 9.2** on the next page).

In the Add Link panel, enter information about your link:

- **Name.** Enter the text of your link in the Name text box. Normal linking-text best practices apply: Make the text descriptive so that people can get an idea of what the link is without having to click it.

- **Web Address.** In this text box, type the URL of the site you want to link to.

note   The Web Address entry must include http:// or https://.

- **Description.** In your travels on the Web, you've hovered over a link or two; we all have. Sometimes some text pops up under your hovering mouse pointer, giving you a little more information about the link. What you enter in the Description text box (an optional setting) is what users see when they hover over the link.

- **Categories**. A link can have as many, or as few, categories as you want to give it. To add one, click the Add New Category link.

 Link categories and post categories are two separate entities, and never the twain shall meet. They're managed and added separately.

Figure 9.2 Enter links in this panel.

Working with advanced settings

All the settings in the Advanced Options panel are optional (**Figure 9.3**), so if you don't want to deal with them, you don't have to.

Figure 9.3 The advanced options are optional.

Here's what these settings do:

- **Target.** Select a Target radio button (**Figure 9.4**) to control how the linked URL opens. _blank opens a new browser window when the link is clicked, _top opens the linked URL in the full browser window (this behavior is obvious only when you are using frames; the link opens in a window of its own), and none opens the linked URL in the current window (or *frameset*).

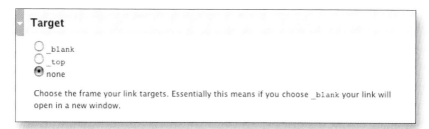

Figure 9.4 Setting the target behavior of the link.

- **Link Relationship (XFN).** I touch on XFN (XHTML Friends Network) in Chapter 6, with regard to posts, but the interface for links (**Figure 9.5**) is much more useful than the interface for posts.

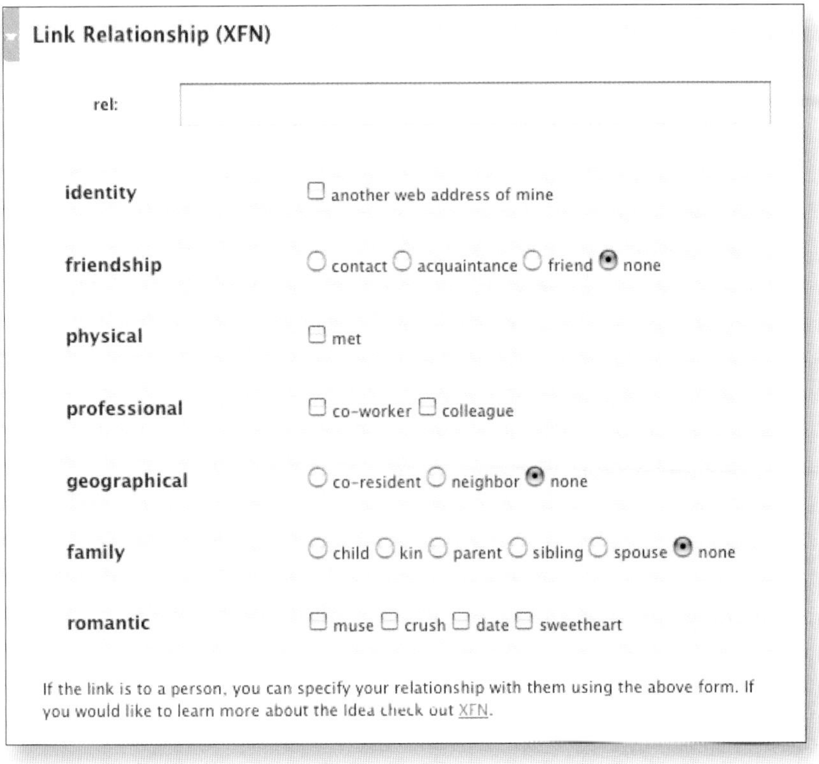

Link Relationship (XFN)

rel:	
identity	☐ another web address of mine
friendship	○ contact ○ acquaintance ○ friend ● none
physical	☐ met
professional	☐ co-worker ☐ colleague
geographical	○ co-resident ○ neighbor ● none
family	○ child ○ kin ○ parent ○ sibling ○ spouse ● none
romantic	☐ muse ☐ crush ☐ date ☐ sweetheart

If the link is to a person, you can specify your relationship with them using the above form. If you would like to learn more about the Idea check out XFN.

Figure 9.5 XFN information encodes your relationship with the owner of the linked blog site.

The table displays the various relationships that XFN can represent. All the options with radio buttons can have only one value, whereas the options with check boxes allow you to select as many values as you like. If I were linking to my own blog, for example, I'd select Another Web Address of Mine in the Identity row and leave it at that. If I were linking to my significant other's blog, however, I'd select Friend in the Friendship row, Met in the Physical row, Co-Resident in the Geographical row, and Sweetheart in the Romantic row (isn't that just too sweet?).

- **Advanced.** It's always fun when advanced options have their own set of advanced options. To give them their due, I give them their own section, which follows.

Moving on up to super-advanced settings

The Advanced settings (**Figure 9.6**) are what I call super-advanced options. (I'll bet that they were reverse-engineered from alien technology.)

Figure 9.6 The advanced advanced options are very, very advanced.

In addition to being super-advanced, these options are very optional. Here's what you can do with them:

- **Image Address.** Some themes are designed to show an image next to the text of the link. (A good image for this purpose is a *favicon*—a little icon that people can make for their Web sites; see the following tip.) If you want to associate an image with the link, enter the image's URL in this text box.

 Find out more about favicons, and make one for your blog, by visiting Steve DeGraeve's Favicon Generator at www.degraeve.com/favicon/.

- **RSS Address.** In this text box, enter the address of the Web site's syndication feed. If you're linking to another WordPress blog, this URL usually is www.*blogname.com*/feed/ (replacing *blogname.com* with the URL of the blog in question, of course).

  For details on RSS, see the nearby sidebar "On Syndication Feeds."

 Some themes make it easy for your readers to subscribe to the blogs in your blogroll by adding the RSS address to the list (based on the value you enter in the RSS Address text box).

On Syndication Feeds

There are a few competing formats in the blogfeedsphere. The two major flavors are Atom and RSS 2.0. (*RSS* stands for *Really Simple Syndication.*) WordPress supports both formats out of the box, so you don't need to worry about support issues.

When you're browsing other people's blogs, though, you may wonder why they choose to use a particular format over another. The short answer is this: The blogger isn't choosing; the vendor of his blogging tool is. I'd say that 98 percent of the bloggers out there don't care which format their feed is in as long as newsreaders can consume it.

Because WordPress supports the two major RSS formats, the vast majority of readers will be able to read your blog.

- **Notes.** At first blush, you may think that notes are just like descriptions (which I cover in "Adding links" earlier in this chapter), but they're not. A description is text that pops up when someone hovers a mouse pointer over the link, whereas the text you enter in the Notes box appears on the page below the link (depending on your WordPress theme, that is; see chapters 11 and 12 for the story on themes).

- **Rating.** You can rate each link from 0 to 9 (0 being no rating and 9 being the highest) by making a choice from the Rating drop-down menu. Most themes don't display rating information, but you can alter a theme to show it (as you can for any of these optional settings), and you can sort links by rating.

Saving your settings

After you've configured all your settings for the link, you need to save those settings. You'll notice a Save button, which you can click to save the link (brilliant!), but right above it is a check box titled Keep This Link Private (**Figure 9.7**). If you check that box before you click Save, WordPress saves the link but doesn't make it visible on your blog. This feature is useful if you want to use your blog as a repository for links you want to remember but don't necessarily want to share with the public.

Figure 9.7 You can keep a link private, if you want.

Importing Links

If you use a newsreader of any kind, you're familiar with OPML. *OPML* (which stands for *Outline Processor Markup Language*) is an XML format that was originally designed for outlines; newsreader vendors have adopted it as a way to get a list of links exported from an application so that your subscription list becomes portable.

It stands to reason that any links you'd want to include in the sidebars of your blog would be in your newsreader, which in turn can export them to an OPML file. WordPress will happily import that OPML file and add those links to your blog. Before you can start using this method to import links, though, you need to have an OPML file on your computer or somewhere on the Internet. You also need to know where that file is so you can supply the location to the Link Importer.

To use this feature, follow these steps:

1. Click the Write link in the navigation bar below your blog's title in the WordPress administrative interface.

2. Click Link to open the Add Links subpanel.

   You'll see Import Links listed in the Related section of the right column.

   or

   Enter this URL: http://*www.yourWordPressURL.com*/wp-admin/link-import.php.

   Either way, the Import Links subpanel opens (**Figure 9.8**).

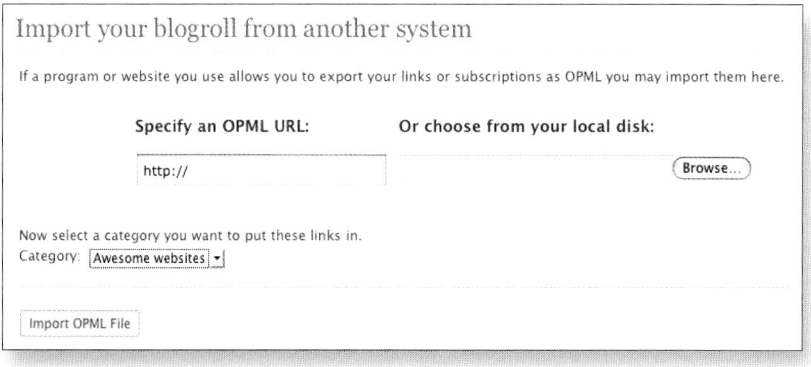

Figure 9.8 The Import Links subpanel.

3. Import your blogroll by typing the URL in the Specify an OPML URL text box, or by clicking the Browse button to find and select an OPML file that you've saved on your computer.

4. From the Category drop-down menu, choose the link category that you want the imported links to go into.

tip

Personally, I put all these links in the Blogroll category.

5. Click the Import OPML File button.

WordPress imports all your links. When it's done, it displays the link names and indicates whether they were inserted (**Figure 9.9**).

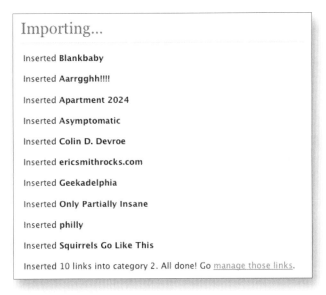

Importing...

Inserted **Blankbaby**

Inserted **Aarrgghh!!!!**

Inserted **Apartment 2024**

Inserted **Asymptomatic**

Inserted **Colin D. Devroe**

Inserted **ericsmithrocks.com**

Inserted **Geekadelphia**

Inserted **Only Partially Insane**

Inserted **philly**

Inserted **Squirrels Go Like This**

Inserted 10 links into category 2. All done! Go manage those links.

Figure 9.9 Importing is all done!

To manage your newly imported links, click the Manage Those Links link. In the next section, I give you some management tips.

Managing Links

As you might expect, you manage links in the Manage Links panel, which is very similar to the Manage Posts panel. You get to the Manage Links panel by choosing Manage > Links or by clicking Manage All Links in the Related section of the Add Link panel (refer to Figure 9.2).

Viewing all your links

The Manage Links panel displays all the links in your blog in a table (**Figure 9.10**). This table contains the following columns:

- **Name.** Edit a link's information by clicking its name.

- **URL.** This column contains a live link to the site in question.

- **Categories.** This column lists all the categories that a link falls into.

- **rel.** The rel column contains any XFN data that you entered for this link (refer to "Working with advanced settings" earlier in this chapter).

- **Visible.** The setting in this column tells you whether the link is private or public (refer to "Saving your settings" earlier in this chapter).

Name	URL	Categories	rel	Visible
Aarrgghh!!!!	numtopia.com/terry/blog	Blogroll		Yes
Apartment 2024	apartment2024.com	Blogroll	friend met co-resident sweetheart	Yes

Figure 9.10 Imported links are also displayed in the Manage Links panel.

Filtering links

As you can in all the other WordPress management panels, you can apply filters to the Manage Links panel to make finding the link you're looking for easier. Just make the appropriate choices from the Category and Order By drop-down menus at the top of the panel.

You can order the results in four ways:

- Order by Link ID
- Order by Address
- Order by Name
- Order by Rating

note Link ID is a unique number that WordPress assigns to each link. This option strikes me as being fairly useless, though.

After you've picked your filter poison, click the Filter button. Then marvel as WordPress displays only the links that you want to see.

Editing and deleting links

Deleting links is just like deleting posts and pages (processes that I cover in Chapter 7 and Chapter 8, respectively). Click the check box next to the link that you want to delete (or Shift-click to select contiguous links) and then click the Delete button. Those links are gone.

Editing links is also quite similar to the posts/pages process. Click the name of the link you want to edit, change the options in the editing panel, and then click the Save button.

Categorizing links

Because they're very different elements, you'll want to organize your links differently from the way you organize posts and pages. WordPress makes this process easy by separating post and page categories from link categories.

Viewing link categories

Choose Manage > Link Categories to open the Manage Link Categories panel, which displays your link categories in a table (**Figure 9.11**).

 note You can't filter these results, so if you have loads of link categories, you may have to do a little bit of scrolling to find the category you're after.

Name	Description	Links
☐ Awesome websites		0
Blogroll		7

Figure 9.11 Link categories.

Along with the category name and description, WordPress displays the number of links in each category. Clicking the number in the Links column takes you to the Manage Links panel, which applies a filter to show only the links in that category.

Deleting a link category

Deleting a link category is straightforward, but note that you can't delete the Blogroll category. You can change its name, however, if you'd rather use that category for a different set of links.

Adding a link category

Clicking the Add New link takes you to the Add Category panel (**Figure 9.12**), which makes it clear that category links are simple compared with their older brothers, plain old categories.

Figure 9.12 The Add Category panel.

You can configure only three settings for a new or existing link category:

- **Category Name.** What you enter in this text box is what WordPress displays as the category name in your links sidebar (depending on your blog's theme).

- **Category Slug.** The Category Slug entry is the URL-friendly version of the category name. Permalinks (see Chapter 5) are based on this slug, so use only lowercase letters, numbers, and hyphens.

- **Description.** Description is the only optional setting. You can enter a description of the link in this text box, but keep it short: Some themes display the description, and overly long descriptions could unbalance the aesthetics of your theme.

When you're done, click the Add Category button (or the Edit Category button, if you're working with an existing link) to save your work and create or edit the link information.

10

Coping with Comments

So far I've covered a few ways for you to create content for your blog: posts, pages, and links. The final piece of the content puzzle is comments.

Comments are a little unusual. You can leave comments on your blog, and so can other people (assuming that you allow comments at all), which means that you have no idea what content other people will create in your blog. Before you freak out, worry not—WordPress offers robust comment management tools that help you separate the wheat from the chaff.

Comments: Bad or Good?

The first decision to make about comments is whether you even want to allow them in your blog. By default, WordPress enables comments globally. This setting is simple enough to change; choose Settings > Discussion to open the Discussion Settings panel (**Figure 10.1**); then clear the Allow People to Post Comments on the Article check box in the Default Article Settings section.

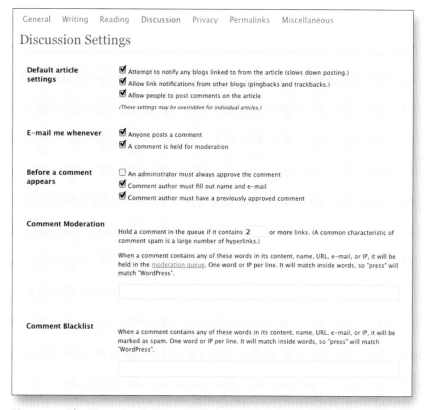

Figure 10.1 The Discussion Settings panel gives you total control of who can comment on your blog.

note If you decide to disable comments globally, you can still enable comments on a post-by-post basis, as I explain in more detail in the "Comments & Pings" section of Chapter 6.

The downside of comments

Why disable comments? Comment spam is the biggest reason. Comment spam, much like normal e-mail spam, attempts to use your blog to advertise a variety of things and to provide links to sites that you probably don't want to be associated with. You can combat this scourge in ways that don't take all the fun of commenting away, however; I talk about those techniques in "Dealing with Comment Spam" later in this chapter.

The other main reason for disabling comments is simple: You aren't interested in what your readers have to say. Some people view a blog as a bully pulpit; their blogs exist only to distribute their messages and don't need to be mucked up with random comments from every Tom, Dick, or Harry.

The upside of comments

The arguments against comments have their place, but I suggest that you think long and hard about the kind of site you want your blog to be. I find that the blogs I enjoy visiting most have a conversational tone, which is enhanced by the opportunity to leave comments and to interact with the poster and fellow readers alike.

Also, blogging is far more interesting when other people comment on your work, because commenting on your own posts is akin to having a discussion with yourself while looking into a mirror. Sure, it's fun for a few minutes, but after a while, you get to thinking that there's more to life than your deep, deep blue eyes.

Who Can Comment

Assuming that I've persuaded you to let people comment on your blog, you have a second decision to make: Which members of the unwashed masses should be able to post a comment on your blog?

Out of the box, WordPress lets anyone comment on your blog, but if that setting is just a little too wide open for your comfort, you can restrict commenting access to those folks who have user accounts on your blog. To restrict comments to users, choose Settings > General to open the

General Settings panel; in the Membership section, click the check box titled Users Must Be Registered and Logged in to Comment; then click the Save Changes button. This method is an effective means of combatting comment spam, and it lowers the risk that people will leave nasty comments on your posts.

This approach has one obvious downside, however: With everyone already having so many accounts and passwords to remember, do you really want to add that extra layer to enable commenting on your blog? You're sure to lose some commenters who aren't interested in signing up for an account just to leave a comment (though the counterargument also stands: If that person's comment isn't worth the effort of creating an account for, it probably isn't worth having).

I'm a proponent of having a devil-may-care attitude toward comments. Let everyone comment; then install a plug-in or two that makes comment spam much more manageable (as I discuss at the end of this chapter). But it's your blog, of course, so it's your choice.

Understanding How Users Comment

Before I delve into how you edit, delete, and generally manage comments in the back end of your blog, I'll explain how people leave comments in the first place.

How unregistered users comment

Figure 10.2 shows a typical comment form for unregistered users of your blog.

Each comment form has four elements:

- Commenter's name
- Commenter's e-mail address
- URL of commenter's Web site (if any)
- Comment text

Leave a Reply

Ambrose	Name (required)
ambrose@example.com	Mail (will not be published) (required)
	Website

Whoever drew that picture is a genius!

Submit Comment

Figure 10.2 The comment form for unregistered users in the default WordPress theme.

The Name and Mail settings are required (though by default, WordPress doesn't display commenters' e-mail addresses). This identification requirement is yet another arrow in your quiver for use against nasty comments; when people have to include their names with their comments, they may be more polite. To cancel this requirement, choose Settings > Discussion to open the Discussion Settings panel; in the Before a Comment Appears section, clear the check box titled Comment Author Must Fill out Name and E-Mail; then click the Save Changes button. When this box is checked, a commenter must enter both her name and e-mail address; when it's cleared, the commenter doesn't have to enter either piece of information.

 note If you check the check box titled Comment Author Must Have a Previously Approved Comment, anyone who's had a comment approved in the past gets a free pass whether or not he's a registered user; his comment skips moderation.

To submit the completed form, the user simply clicks the Submit Comment button.

When users are required to provide both their names and e-mail addresses, and someone tries to enter a comment without providing that information, WordPress displays an error message. WordPress also displays error messages when a user tries to submit a blank comment or submits several comments in rapid succession—behaviors that are typical of programs that leave comment spam. That user is blocked for a few minutes; after that period is up, the user can comment again.

How registered users comment

If a logged-in registered user wants to comment, he sees a slightly different comment form (**Figure 10.3**). All the user has to do is enter his comment in the text box and click the Submit Comment button. Because the user is already logged in, WordPress already knows who he is, so it doesn't need to ask for identity information again.

Figure 10.3 The comment form for logged-in users.

> **tip** A logged-in user can click her name in the comment form to edit her profile information (see Chapter 3).

Moderating Comments

After a user submits a comment, depending on the blog's settings, either he sees his comment on the post along with the message *Your comment is awaiting moderation* (**Figure 10.4**), or the comment is published immediately.

Figure 10.4 A posted comment awaiting moderation.

You may wonder how WordPress can display a comment that is awaiting moderation to the person who left it while hiding it from everyone else. The answer is quite simple: magic. OK, not really, but it seems like magic, doesn't it? WordPress uses browser cookies to keep track of who is looking at the blog. Thanks to the cookies, WordPress can display certain content, such as comments, to certain people.

Moderation is your job as an administrator, as I discuss in the following sections.

Comment tests

Before you see any comments, WordPress tests all comments that people submit to your blog and runs a few tests on them, based on the following information:

- **Identity requirements.** I discuss these settings in "How unregistered users comment" earlier in this chapter.

- **Comment contents.** WordPress also considers the Comment Moderation settings in the Discussion panel. If a comment has more than a certain number of links (the default setting is 2, but you can set as many as you want) or contains any word, Internet Protocol (IP) address, e-mail address, or URL that you list, that comment is held for moderation. See Chapter 5 for more information.

- **Blacklist.** WordPress checks to see whether the comment is spam based on the settings in the Comment Blacklist section of the Discussion panels. If any content that you list in this section appears in a comment, WordPress marks it as spam. Comments that are identified as spam don't get published to your blog. There's one exception: A registered user can leave a comment with blacklisted items in it. Registered users generally are people you trust, so it makes sense that WordPress trusts them as well.

 Depending on what plug-ins you have installed, those plug-ins may also scan comments before they are cleared or marked as spam. (See Chapter 13 for more information about plug-ins.)

If a comment passes all these tests, WordPress sends it to the moderation queue and alerts you (as the administrator) that the comment is waiting for moderation.

Comment alerts

When WordPress sends a comment to moderation, it's asking a human (that is, an administrator of the blog) to look at the comment and give it thumbs-up or thumbs-down. By default, WordPress sends you, via e-mail, the text of each comment that ends up in the moderation queue.

The e-mail that you receive is pretty darned concise and useful. The post title is in the Subject line of the email, along with the phrase *Please moderate* (which allows you to create some mail rules to organize your e-mail, if that's your bag).

The body of the message includes a link to the blog post that received the comment, as well as some information about the comment:

- **Author.** This line lists the comment's author, the IP address of the computer she sent the comment from, and a reverse lookup on that address.

- **Email.** This line provides the commenter's e-mail address, if you require it (refer to "How unregistered users comment" earlier in this chapter).

- **URL.** If the commenter provided a URL, it appears in this line.

- **Whois.** This line is link to a Whois lookup on the commenter's IP address, which returns some information about the commenter's location.

- **Comment.** This line contains the comment text.

 tip   I find this notification feature to be very handy, but if you'd rather not get the e-mails, simply choose Settings > Discussion to open the Discussion Settings panel; clear the check box titled Email Me Whenever a Comment Is Held for Moderation; and then click the Save Changes button.

Below all that information are four links that let you act on the comment. I discuss these actions in the following sections.

Comment actions

The bottom of a comment-notification e-mail from WordPress provides links to four separate actions you can take on the pending comment.

Approve the comment

To approve the comment, click the Approve It link. That link takes you to a confirmation panel (**Figure 10.5**) that asks whether you're sure you want to approve the comment. Click No or Approve Comment. If you click No, the comment remains in the moderation queue.

Caution: You are about to approve the following comment:	
Are you sure you want to do that?	
No	Approve Comment
Author	Ambrose
E-mail	ambrose@example.com
Comment	Whoever drew that picture is a genius!

Figure 10.5 Confirm comment approval in this panel.

Delete the comment

If the comment is obviously spam or is otherwise objectionable, you can delete the comment by clicking the Delete It link. A confirmation panel asks whether you're sure you want to delete the comment (**Figure 10.6**). Click No to cancel or Delete Comment to delete the comment.

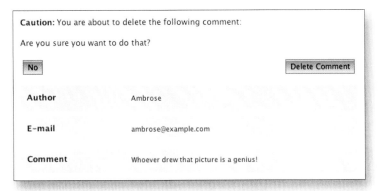

Figure 10.6 Confirm comment deletion in this panel.

Mark the comment as spam

Instead of deleting a comment outright, you can mark it as spam by clicking the Spam It link in the notification e-mail. Again, a confirmation panel asks you to confirm your choice (**Figure 10.7**); click No or Spam Comment.

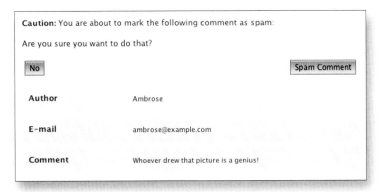

Figure 10.7 Confirming that you want to mark a comment as spam.

Unlike deleting a comment, marking a comment as spam doesn't delete it from the WordPress database. Instead, WordPress holds on to the comment in the hope that you'll activate a comment-spam plug-in, so that it can add the comment to a central spam-comment database (see "Dealing with Comment Spam" later in this chapter).

Manage the comment

The final link in the e-mail takes you to the Manage Comments panel, which applies a filter to display only moderated comments. That panel is the topic of the following section.

Managing Comments

All roads lead to comment management, it seems. You can get to the Manage Comments panel in several ways:

- **Right Now bar.** When you log in to the Dashboard, right below the orange Right Now bar, WordPress displays the number of comments awaiting moderation (**Figure 10.8**). Click the link for those comments to open the Manage Comments panel, filtered to show only comments awaiting moderation. (To open the panel in an unfiltered state, click the link for total comments instead.)

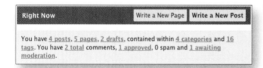

Figure 10.8 The Right Now bar gives you instant access to comment statistics.

- **E-mail link.** You can click the "moderation panel" link in the comment notification e-mail (refer to the preceding section) to get to the Manage Comments panel.

- **Comments link.** The navigation bar in the administrator interface contains a Comments link that takes you to the Manage Comments panel. When comments are waiting for moderation, a little speech bubble containing the number of waiting comments appears to the right of the Comments link (**Figure 10.9**).

Figure 10.9 A red speech bubble alerts to you to new comments.

Viewing comments

Comment management is just like link, post, and page management, in that you do everything through a management panel—in this case, Manage Comments (**Figure 10.10**).

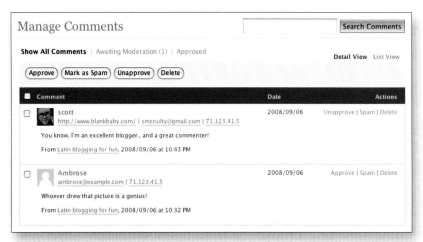

Figure 10.10 The Manage Comments panel looks very much like the Manage Pages and Manage Posts panels.

This panel lists all the comments on your blog in a nice table with the following columns:

- **Comment.** This wide column displays the commenter's name, avatar (where appropriate), name, URL, and e-mail and IP addresses; the comment itself; and a link to the post on which the comment was made.

- **Date.** This column lists the date when the comment was made.

- **Actions.** In this column, you see the actions you can take on the comment: Approve (if it hasn't been approved yet) or Unapprove (if the comment was approved but is unblogworthy), Spam, and Delete.

 note   If you click the Unapprove link, you don't delete the comment; you just take it down from the post.

You can use either of two views in the Manage Comments panel. The default, detail view, shows you all the comment details you could want. But if you switch to list view by clicking the List View link in the top-right corner of the panel, the view changes slightly. You no longer see the text of the comment—just some information about the commenter and what post that person commented on (**Figure 10.11**). All the actions are still available to you, however.

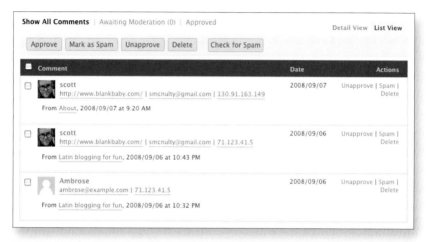

Figure 10.11 The Manage Comments panel in list view.

Deciphering the Manage Comments Panel

Astute readers may have noticed that the background of the Manage Comments panel is two different colors in Figure 10.10 earlier in this chapter. The bottom comment, which is awaiting moderation, has a light yellow background. The alternating yellow and white backgrounds (white for approved comments) help you see easily how many posts you need to approve.

The number of comments awaiting moderation is also displayed at the top of the Manage Comments panel, next to the Awaiting Moderation link. Click that link, and WordPress filters the panel to show only comments that need to be moderated. You can also show all comments or only approved comments by clicking the appropriate links.

Managing comments in batches

Approving and rejecting comments individually works well enough when you have one or two comments. But what if you have several hundred comments that need to be approved?

The Manage Comments panel displays 20 comments at a time. You'll notice a check box next to each comment. Click the check boxes of the comments on which you want to execute the bulk action (or Shift-click to select contiguous comments); then click one of the four buttons at the top of the panel: Approve, Mark As Spam, Unapprove, or Delete.

WordPress performs the action instantly, and then you can move on to work on the next batch of 20 comments.

Searching for comments

When you have a large number of comments, searching becomes important. As you can in the management panels for posts, pages, and links, you can type a search term in the search text box and click the Search Comments button. WordPress returns all comments that meet your search criteria (**Figure 10.12**).

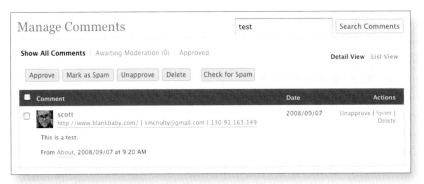

Figure 10.12 A search for test returns one comment.

tip   You can also click the IP address listed with the comment to show only comments sent from the computer with that IP address. This feature is useful when you get several identical comments from a bunch of seemingly different people.

If you notice a large number of comments coming from the same IP address but being submitted under different names, one of two things could be going on:

- Someone is leaving comments under false names.

- Your blog is popular with residents of a single household who use the same router to connect to the Internet.

Either way, this is a good trick to figure out who is leaving comments on your blog.

Editing comments

Your blog is your kingdom, so you get to make the rules. You decide who can (and can't) comment, post, and otherwise enjoy your blog.

 Your absolute rule extends to the contents of comments, but a word of warning: With great power comes great responsibility. Why do I mention responsibility? You should think twice before altering words that someone else wrote. Fixing grammatical errors or censoring swear words is one thing, but I, for one, would never want to change the meaning of someone else's comments.

Clicking a commenter's name in the Manage Comments panel takes you to the Edit Comment dialog box (**Figure 10.13** on the next page), where you can change just about everything related to the comment:

- **Name.** You can change the name that the comment was left under by typing a new name in this text box. In the past, folks have e-mailed me asking that I change their name on some comments on one of my blogs, and this setting is how I did it.

- **E-Mail.** You can change the e-mail address associated with a comment as well by typing a new address in this text box.

 Most WordPress themes don't display commenters' e-mail addresses on the blog itself, so that spam bots can't harvest addresses. (For information on themes, see chapters 11 and 12.)

- **URL.** Type a new address in this text box to change the URL.

Figure 10.13 To edit a comment, just click the commenter's name in the Comment Management panel. You can change anything you want.

- **Comment.** This section is where you enter potentially dangerous territory. You can format the comment by using some familiar HTML tools (check out Chapter 6 to find out what these tools do). You can also change the comment's text, leaving no outward sign that a change has been made.

- **View This Comment.** This feature works only on comments that have been approved. Click this button to go directly to the comment itself. (Each comment has its own permalink, which is based on the permalink of the post.)

- **Approval Status.** The Approval Status drop-down menu contains three options: Moderated, Approved, and Spam.

- **Time.** You can edit the time stamp on the comment by clicking the Edit link next to the current time stamp.

- **Save** and **Delete Comment.** Clicking the Save button saves all your changes; clicking the Delete Comment link deletes the comment.

- **Related.** Two links—Manage All Comments and Moderate Comments—round out the options in the Edit Comment dialog box.

Dealing with Comment Spam

I've mentioned comment spam more than a few times already, because it's a big problem. For very little money, people can program small applications (called *bots*) to search the Internet for blogs and leave comments full of links to various sites of ill repute. Luckily, WordPress now ships with a plug-in that can really help your fight against comment and trackback spam. (For more on trackbacks, check out Chapter 5.)

The Akismet plug-in—made by Automattic, which also created WordPress.com—adds a step to the comment-vetting process. When a comment is submitted to a blog that's running Akismet, the Akismet Web service runs several tests on that comment, comparing it with known spam comments in a large database. These tests run very quickly. Then Akismet marks the comment as spam if it meets the criteria or passes it along to the next step in the comment system. (Depending on how you have your blog set up, that next step usually is the moderation or publishing queue. See Chapter 5 for help on deciding whether to moderate your comments.)

You don't know it yet, but you're going to love this plug-in.

Activating the Akismet plug-in

Activating Akismet is easy. Click Plugins, and you'll see two listed in the Inactive Plugins section (**Figure 10.14**). In the Action column for each plug-in, you see two links: Activate and Edit. Click Activate in the Akismet row, and you'll be notified that you need a WordPress API key to enable Akismet.

Figure 10.14 Activating Akismet is as simple as clicking the Activate link and providing your API key.

This API (application programming interface) key is a way for the people at Akismet to track the sources of spam comments. Getting a key may seem like an annoyance, but the key is used to log which comments are being reported as spam. This tracking ensures that legitimate comments aren't being identified as spam for nefarious purposes (and vice versa).

To get an API key, you need to sign up for a profile at WordPress.com. (Don't worry; it's free.) After you get your profile, click Edit Profile, which is listed in the My Account section. This link takes you to your profile on WordPress.com. Your API key (which you shouldn't share with anyone) is listed right below the header Your Profile and Personal Options.

After you enter your API key, you have one more decision to make: whether you want Akismet to discard spam comments on posts more than a month old (**Figure 10.15**). By default, this option is disabled, which means that spam comments on posts older than a month are treated just like any other potential spam comments: marked as spam and held in a queue for 15 days. If you don't mark them as not spam, the comments are deleted after 15 days.

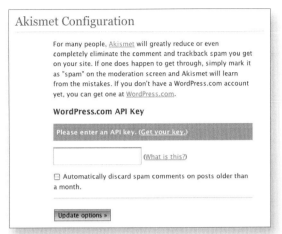

Figure 10.15 The Akismet Configuration dialog box.

The Cost of Akismet

Akismet is a great plug-in and a bargain at any price, if you ask me. Luckily, Automattic gives Akismet away to the vast majority of users. If you're using Akismet for only one or two blogs, you don't need to pay anything.

A few paid options are available, though, offering the usual benefits:

- Paid accounts have priority over free accounts in the form of getting access to new versions first. Requests for paid accounts are handled by the Web service before free account requests (though the difference isn't noticeable).

- Traffic is never throttled for paid accounts. The Akismet Web service may check free accounts for spam less frequently, however, if those free accounts generate lots of requests.

- Paid users get notified first when an update is out.

If you make more than $500 a month from your blogs, you may want to opt for a pro-blogger API key. For $5 a month, you get access to all the benefits described above and also technical support against comment spam.

Enterprise customers (big companies) can sign up for enterprise-level accounts, and discounts are available for not-for-profit organizations.

Check out http://akismet.com/commercial for all the pricing details.

If you change your mind about these settings or want to use your API key for another blog, you can change these settings at any time by choosing Plugins > Akismet Configuration (a command that's available only when the Akismet plug-in is active).

Viewing the spam queue

After you activate Akismet, when you go back to the Manage Comments panel (by clicking the Comments tab in the navigation bar below your blog's title in the WordPress administrative interface), you'll notice a new Akismet Spam link below the top navigation bar (**Figure 10.16**).

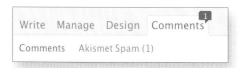

Figure 10.16 A new Akismet Spam link, which appears when the Akismet plug-in is activated.

Clicking that link takes you to the Caught Spam panel, which shows your spam queue. This is where you go to see all the spam that has been caught and to make sure that no valid comments have been wrongly accused. The panel shown in **Figure 10.17** has only one lonely spam comment, but that number will grow the longer the blog is online.

The handy Delete All button deletes every spam comment in the queue, no matter how many there are. WordPress doesn't ask you to confirm each individual deletion, so make sure that you want to delete all the spam comments before you click that button.

You can display the Caught Spam panel in any of three views—All (both spam comments and trackbacks), Comments (comments only), and Trackbacks (spam trackbacks only)—by clicking the appropriate link. (Figure 10.17 shows only one spam comment, so the only link allows you to filter by comments. If the account had some trackback spam, you'd see an additional link to filter by trackbacks.) You can also search your spam queue for any legitimate comments that may have found their way into the wrong virtual neighborhood.

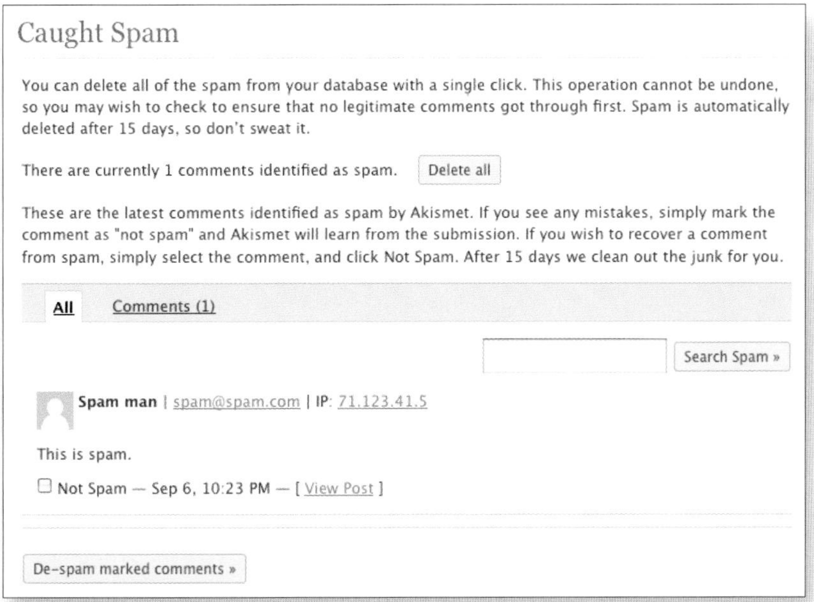

Caught Spam

You can delete all of the spam from your database with a single click. This operation cannot be undone, so you may wish to check to ensure that no legitimate comments got through first. Spam is automatically deleted after 15 days, so don't sweat it.

There are currently 1 comments identified as spam.   Delete all

These are the latest comments identified as spam by Akismet. If you see any mistakes, simply mark the comment as "not spam" and Akismet will learn from the submission. If you wish to recover a comment from spam, simply select the comment, and click Not Spam. After 15 days we clean out the junk for you.

All   Comments (1)

Search Spam »

Spam man | spam@spam.com | IP: 71.123.41.5

This is spam.

☐ Not Spam — Sep 6, 10:23 PM — [View Post]

De-spam marked comments »

Figure 10.17 The Caught Spam panel.

De-spamming messages entails clicking the Not Spam check box for each comment or trackback that should have its reputation cleansed. After you've selected all the messages that you want to de-spam, click the De-Spam Marked Comments link; WordPress takes them out of the spam queue.

11

Working with Themes and Widgets

You may have noticed that I've mentioned WordPress themes in the preceding chapters but haven't really explained what they are. Like a clever tech writer, I was saving all that good information for this chapter.

Themes determine the look of your blog and save you the bother of having to deal with most of the code involved—though if you're interested in that sort of thing, WordPress allows you to get your hands into as much code as you like. Most people will be happy keeping the default WordPress theme, which is known simply as WordPress Default 1.6 (though some people still use its former moniker, Kubrick).

Viewing the Current Theme

The default download of WordPress includes two themes: the default version and WordPress Classic. (Classic was the default theme before WordPress 1.2.) To see what themes you have installed, click the Design tab in the WordPress admin navigation bar, directly below your blog title. WordPress takes you right to the Themes panel (**Figure 11.1**).

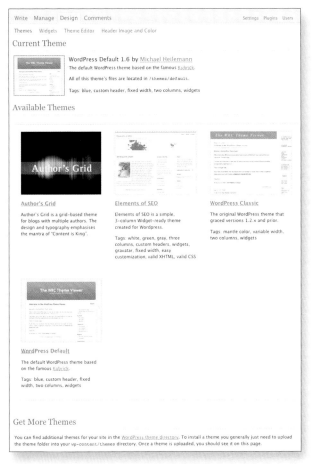

Figure 11.1 The Themes panel lists all the themes you have installed. This example shows a few themes installed in addition to the default theme.

The first thing you see is a thumbnail of the active theme in the Current Theme section (**Figure 11.2**). This theme, the one that's applied to your blog right now, is responsible for the look and feel of your blog. The Current Theme section also displays the theme's name, a link to the author's site, a brief description, and some tags.

Figure 11.2 When you're in the Themes panel, finding your current theme is easy.

Viewing the default theme's tags and options

Posts aren't the only things that are tagged in WordPress (see Chapter 10 for more information about tags and posts). Themes are also tagged. Unlike a post, though, a theme includes tags to let users know something about the theme without having to apply it. The default theme, for example, has the following tags: blue, custom header, fixed width, two columns, and widgets. These tags tell you that that the predominant color of this theme is blue, that you can customize the header, that the theme has a fixed width (it doesn't resize with the browser window) and two columns, and that it supports widgets.

Some themes have additional options, and WordPress displays links for those options in the navigation bar at the top of the Themes panel (**Figure 11.3**). The default theme, for example, adds an option called Header Image and Color, which allows you to customize the color of the header graphic and make your blog stand out a little from the crowd.

Themes   Widgets   Theme Editor   Header Image and Color

Figure 11.3 The Themes panel's navigation bar. Header Image and Color won't be listed for every theme, however.

Customizing the default theme's header

To customize the header in the default theme, follow these steps:

1. Click the Header Image and Color link in the Themes panel's navigation bar.

   The Header Image and Color dialog box opens (**Figure 11.4**).

Figure 11.4 The Header Image and Color dialog box.

2. Click one of the three color buttons: Font Color, Upper Color, or Lower Color.

   The Color Picker opens (**Figure 11.5**).

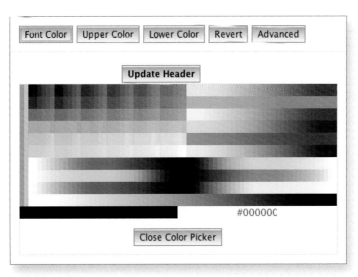

Figure 11.5 All the (Web-safe) colors of the rainbow are available to you.

note The Upper Color and Lower Color settings allow you to create a gradient effect in the header. Upper blends into Lower. If you want your header to be a solid color, assign the same value to the Upper Color and Lower Color settings.

3. Click a color you like, or click the Advanced button to enter code values (**Figure 11.6**).

   If you choose the Advanced option, enter a CSS (Cascading Style Sheets) value in the Font Color text box and hexadecimal codes in the Upper Color and Lower Color text boxes.

Figure 11.6 If you're a hardcore geek, you can enter code for your colors.

 tip CSS and hex colors are beyond the scope of this book, but for more information, check out *CSS, DHTML, and Ajax, Fourth Edition: Visual QuickStart Guide,* by Jason Cranford Teague (Peachpit Press).

4. Click the Update Header button.

tip If your color choice turns out to be particularly hideous, click the Revert button in the Color Picker to go back to the default color scheme.

5. When you're happy with the result, click the Close Color Picker button.

 note Not every theme has an option like this one. Check the theme's documentation to be sure.

Changing the theme

You don't have to stick with the default WordPress theme, though. You can change your blog's theme in several ways:

- Install and apply a different theme

- Add some widgets (if the theme supports them) to add more content

- Edit the current theme to add or subtract features

In the rest of the chapter, I cover each method in turn. By the end of this chapter, you'll be able to tweak stock themes and make them just what you want.

Installing a New Theme

Every WordPress uses the same default theme when it's installed, and this theme is a nice one, but how boring would the blogosphere be if all blogs looked alike? That's where themes come it. A new theme is like a new coat of paint for your blog, making it stand out from the crowd.

Lots of people make themes available for download on the Web; all you have to do is find them, download them, and then install them. In this section, I show you how to do exactly that.

Finding a new theme

The WordPress community makes several great add-ons. A whole army of people out there, with much better taste than little old me, are hard at work creating WordPress themes. All they ask (usually) is that you link back to them on your blog. Chapter 12 lists several Web sites that offer themes of all types for your blog.

Installing the theme files

The first step in installing a new theme is downloading the files to your computer. The files will be compressed in an archive, such as a .zip file. When you've downloaded the archive, use your favorite decompression utility to expand it. Then transfer the theme folder via FTP to the themes directory on the remote server that hosts your blog:

www.*yourWordPressURL*.com/wp-content/themes

After you've uploaded the new theme's folder, refresh the Themes panel to verify that the theme is installed and ready to use.

Applying the new theme

The Available Themes section of the Themes panel shows thumbnails of all the themes that are currently installed (**Figure 11.7**).

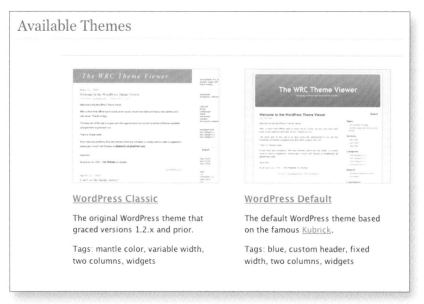

Figure 11.7 The Available Themes section, displaying thumbnail previews of installed themes.

Click either the thumbnail or the theme link to preview a theme. The great thing about this preview is that it shows you what the actual contents of your blog would look like in the selected theme (**Figure 11.8**). This feature saves a lot of time when you're trying to decide among several themes.

Activate link

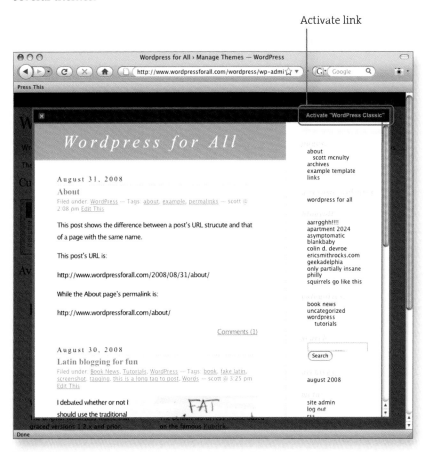

Figure 11.8 Clicking a theme shows you what your blog will look like with that theme applied.

When you find the theme you want to use, click the Activate link in the preview window. WordPress applies the new theme to your blog and displays an alert window with a Visit Site link to your blog, so you can see how the blog looks in its new duds.

Adding Widgets for Code-Free Customization

If the thought of mucking around with code makes your skin crawl, worry not. Widgets let you customize your WordPress theme without writing a single line of code.

To use widgets, you need a theme that supports them, which means a theme that has sections defined as sidebars. Finding out whether your current theme supports widgets is very easy: Check the navigation bar of the Themes panel for a Widgets link. Click that link, and you'll be taken to the Widgets panel of the current theme. If that theme doesn't support widgets, you'll see an error message with a link to some WordPress documentation about making your theme widget compatible (**Figure 11.9**). That caveat aside, lots of themes support widgets, and they really do make customization easy.

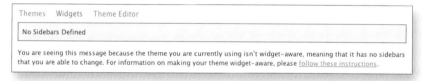

Themes   Widgets   Theme Editor

No Sidebars Defined

You are seeing this message because the theme you are currently using isn't widget-aware, meaning that it has no sidebars that you are able to change. For information on making your theme widget-aware, please follow these instructions.

Figure 11.9 Widgets can be used only with themes that have defined sidebars. If your theme doesn't have at least one sidebar defined, you'll see this error.

Viewing widgets

To view your widgets, click the Widgets link in the Themes panel. The Widgets panel opens, listing the widgets that come installed with WordPress (**Figure 11.10** on the next page).

You can view this list in any of three ways—Show All Widgets, Show Unused Widgets (only those widgets that aren't currently in use), and Show Used Widgets—by choosing a view from the drop-down menu at the top of the panel. You can also search for widgets, which is handy when you have more than 20 or so of them installed.

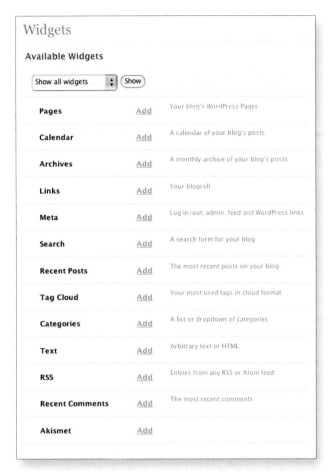

Figure 11.10 The Widgets panel, displaying the default widgets available in a fresh WordPress installation. (Note that because the Akismet plug-in is activated, the Akismet widget is available.)

Viewing sidebars

In the Current Widgets section on the right side of the panel, a drop-down menu lists the sidebars—the areas of the theme in which widgets can appear (**Figure 11.11**). The default WordPress theme has only one area that can display widgets: Sidebar 1. In a fresh WordPress installation, Sidebar 1 contains no custom widgets.

If the current theme has multiple sidebars, you can select any sidebar by choosing it from the drop-down menu and then clicking the Show button.

Figure 11.11 At the moment, Sidebar 1 doesn't have any widgets.

Applying widgets

Widgets don't have an installation process of their own, because they're actually specialized plug-ins (or additional parts of traditional plug-ins) that add functions to your sidebar. You install widgets by installing plug-ins that exist solely to add widgets or that have companion widgets in addition to other features. I cover this topic in more detail in Chapter 13.

To add a widget to the selected sidebar (refer to the preceding section), follow these steps:

1. In the Available Widgets section of the Widgets panel, find the widget you want to use, and click its Add link.

   A blue bar representing the widget appears in the Current Widgets section, with an Edit link in the bar. (I discuss this link in "Reordering and removing widgets" later in the chapter.)

2. Repeat Step 1 for each widget you want to add (**Figure 11.12**).

Figure 11.12 Adding two widgets: Pages and Calendar.

3. Click the Save Changes button.

You've just added widgets to your blog. Not that hard, huh?

Setting widget options

Each widget has some options that change the way it behaves. Changing these options is easy. On the right side of the Widgets panel is a Current Widgets column, which lists the widgets that are currently applied to your blog. You can change the settings only for widgets that are applied to your blog. Click the Edit link of the applied widget that you want to change, and WordPress displays the settings information for that widget. In the following sections, I discuss what each widget does and how you can customize it to suit your needs.

Pages

If you've created a bunch of pages, this widget can display a list of those pages. You can give the widget a new title (perhaps Sections), set sorting options, and create an exclusion list (**Figure 11.13**). You can exclude pages based on their IDs, separated by commas.

Figure 11.13 The Pages widget displays your blog's pages based on the criteria you set.

 To get a page's ID, choose Manage > Pages to open the Manage Pages panel; then click the page's name. At the end of the URL, you see something like post=2. The number is the page's ID number.

Calendar

Blogs are largely time based, so it makes sense that you can display a calendar of your posts. The Calendar widget allows you to show a month at a time; in the calendar that appears in your blog, each day on which you made a post is a link to that day's posts (**Figure 11.14**). The only option you can change in the widget is Title.

		August 2008				
M	T	W	T	F	S	S
				1	2	3
4	5	6	7	8	9	10
11	12	13	14	15	16	17
18	19	20	21	22	23	24
25	26	27	28	29	30	31

Figure 11.14 The output of the Calendar widget.

Archives

Older entries don't just disappear into the ether; they live on in the archives. The Archives widget (**Figure 11.15**) displays a link to your archives in the sidebar. The archive is shown as a monthly list, and you can display the post count next to the month.

Figure 11.15 The Archives widget.

tip If you have a large archive, you may want to check the Display As a Drop Down check box so that the widget takes up less space.

Links

The Links widget displays a list of your links (**Figure 11.16**). You can't exclude anything or set any other options.

Awesome websites

» WordPress For All

Blogroll

» Aarrgghh!!!!
» Apartment 2024
» Asymptomatic
» Blankbaby
» Colin D. Devroe
» ericsmithrocks.com
» Geekadelphia
» Only Partially Insane
» philly
» Squirrels Go Like This

Figure 11.16 The Links widget displays all your links and groups them by link category.

Meta

The Meta widget displays a collection of links about WordPress itself (**Figure 11.17**), including a link to your WordPress login page, a logout link (if you're logged in), and a link to WordPress.org. You can change the display name of this widget, but that's about it.

Meta

» Site Admin
» Log out
» Entries RSS
» Comments RSS
» WordPress.org

Figure 11.17 The Meta widget adds several WordPress-related links.

Search

This widget adds a search control to the sidebar (**Figure 11.18**). It has no options you can set.

Figure 11.18 The Search widget gives your sidebar a search feature.

Recent Posts

You can showcase 1 to 15 of your latest posts in your sidebar with the Recent Posts widget (**Figure 11.19**). The widget displays the titles of the posts as links to those posts. You can change the title of this widget.

Figure 11.19 You can set the Recent Posts widget to display up to 15 of your latest posts.

Tag Cloud

The Tag Cloud widget is useful only if you tag your posts. (For information on tagging posts, see Chapter 6.) A *tag cloud* is a visual representation of all the tags you use in your blog; the more posts are tagged with a particular word, the larger that word is displayed (**Figure 11.20**). Each tag in the cloud is a link that allows you to search for all posts tagged in that manner. You can change the title of this widget.

Figure 11.20 Tag clouds are all the rage nowadays, and the Tag Cloud widget lets you get in on the fun.

Categories

The Categories widget (**Figure 11.21**) is much like the Pages widget: It displays all your categories in a list or a drop-down menu. You can also display the number of posts in each category. Finally, if you use parent categories, you can reflected that fact in this widget by enabling the Show Hierarchy option, which indents subcategories below their parent categories.

Figure 11.21 The Categories widget displays categories as links in your sidebar.

Text

The Text widget (**Figure 11.22**) is the most customizable of all. You can change the title of the widget and enter any text in the body that you want to put in it. You could add a bio of yourself or some code to embed a video, for example.

Figure 11.22 The Text widget.

RSS

The RSS widget (**Figure 11.23**) displays the last 1 to 20 posts of a given RSS feed in your sidebar. By default, it shows only headlines that link back to the full post, but you can set it to display item content, item author, and the date of the post.

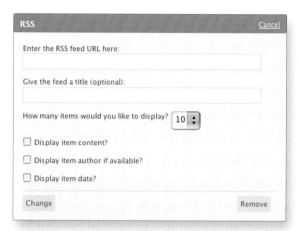

Figure 11.23 The RSS widget displays the contents of any RSS feed that you give it.

Recent Comments

As you may have picked up on by this point, I'm a fan of comments. I'm also a fan of the Recent Comments widget, which displays the latest comments that have been left on your blog—up to 15. **Figure 11.24** shows this widget in action.

Figure 11.24 Blogs are conversations, and the Recent Comments widget encourages conversation by highlighting the most recent comments on your blog.

Akismet

This simple widget becomes available as soon as you activate the Akismet plug-in (see Chapter 10). The Akismet widget shows you how many spam comments the plug-in has caught so far (**Figure 11.25**). You can change the title of this widget, which doubles as a link to http://akismet.com.

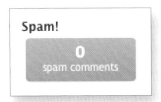

Figure 11.25 The Akismet widget displays the number of spam comments Akismet has caught.

Reordering and removing widgets

Getting rid of a widget that no longer floats your boat is a breeze. In the Current Widgets section of the Widgets panel (refer to "Applying widgets" earlier in this chapter), click the extraneous widget's Edit link; then click the Remove button in the bottom-right corner of the widget. This procedure takes the widget off the sidebar.

note Don't forget to save your changes by clicking the Save Changes button.

You may be happy with the widgets that you have in your sidebar, but maybe not with the order in which they appear. To reorder widgets, just drag and drop them into new positions in the Available Widgets list (**Figure 11.26**); then click Save Changes to update your sidebar.

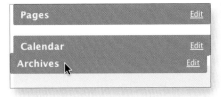

Figure 11.26 Reordering widgets is as simple as dragging and dropping.

Customizing the Current Theme

Widgets are great ways to make a theme all your own without digging into the actual code of a theme. There are limits to what widgets alone can do, though, and as you become a more advanced WordPress user, you'll run into some of those limits. Luckily, with just a small amount of code editing you can really change the look and functionality of themes.

Suppose that you've applied the Author's Grid theme (refer to "Installing the theme files" earlier in this chapter) but don't care for the big gray square on the right side (**Figure 11.27**). Luckily, you can replace it with something more to your liking.

Figure 11.27 My blog with the Author's Grid theme applied. You may want to get rid of that big gray box.

Customizing a theme requires you to edit the files that make up the theme itself. You can work with the files in either of two ways:

- Use your favorite text editor to edit the files in the theme directory.

- Use the built-in Theme Editor feature of WordPress to handle the editing duties.

In the following sections, I discuss both methods.

Editing the theme files manually

If you look inside one of your themes' folders, you'll find a variety of files in there. Some, like index.php and page.php, are templates that provide a consistent structure to the content that they display via template tags (which I discuss in Chapter 12). The actual content varies from theme to theme, but most themes have the following basic building blocks:

- **index.php.** This file rules them all. The index file, in Web speak, is the default document. When you visit a Web site (www.wordpressforall. com, for example), what you don't notice is that the Web server is automatically serving up the index.php file. That file contains all the logic needed to present your blog. Without this file, your blog won't work at all. The index.php file contains the logic that controls how your posts are displayed. You can change where the date and author are displayed, tweak the navigation, or have the index display only certain posts by means of a filter.

- **style.css.** You may have other .css files in addition to this one, but style.css will definitely be there. CSS (Cascading Style Sheets) uses nifty little text files to specify the physical appearance of your blog. The templates (such as index.php) provide the structure of your blog; CSS provides the paint and wallpaper that make your blog a nice place to hang out.

- **header.php** and **footer.php.** Computers are good at a great many things, chief among them saving us poor saps some time here and there. All the pages of your blog have a few common characteristics, including a header graphic, a navigation bar, and a footer with copyright information. The header.php and footer.php files hold header and footer information. When you need to change either the header or the footer, just edit this file; WordPress applies the change to your entire blog.

- **page.php** and **single.php.** Both of these files are templates for content types. The page.php file is the default page template, and single.php is the template for posts. (Whenever someone visits a post's permalink, she's actually visiting single.php.) If you change the index.php file to alter the way posts are displayed, you need to make the same changes in the single.php file. (You can make the same changes in both files, but WordPress doesn't automatically apply the changes from one file to the other.)

- **sidebar.php.** A blog without a sidebar is hardly a blog at all—at least, that's the way it feels these days. The sidebar has become an essential part of every blog, used to display anything from the proprietor's bio to a blogroll to pictures. The sidebar.php file is responsible for how the sidebar looks.

- **comments.php.** This file that determines how comments are displayed for a post and what the comment form looks like. If you want to change any of the form labels, this file is the place to do it.

- **404.php.** A 404 error occurs when you point your browser to a page that no longer exists (or didn't exist to begin with). When the browser asks a Web server for something that doesn't exist, the server has nothing to show, so it returns a 404 error message. The 404.php file is a custom 404 error that you can make a little more useful with some tweaking. Instead of just saying that the page doesn't exist, you could serve up a search page so that your visitor can look for an answer instead of navigating away in frustration.

- **screenshot.png.** After you install a theme, a helpful screen shot appears in the Themes panel to give you a sense of what the theme looks like. The screenshot.png file is the image that WordPress displays. If a screen shot doesn't show up for a newly installed theme, make sure that the theme's folder contains a file with this name.

- **functions.php.** *Functions* are pieces of code that do particular tasks. Programmers place a bunch of these functions in a central place so that other parts of their code can access them. In WordPress, some themes have their own functions that are contained in the functions. php file. Looking at this file is fine, but unless you know a thing or two about PHP, I suggest that you leave it alone (or at least make a backup of the file before you change it).

Editing the theme with Theme Editor

Because this book is about WordPress (in case you haven't noticed by now), you may as well use the built-in tool.

Working with Theme Editor

To open Theme Editor, click the Theme Editor link in the Themes panel. You see a list of your theme's files on the right side of the window; the scrolling pane on the left side of the window displays the code of the selected file (**Figure 11.28**).

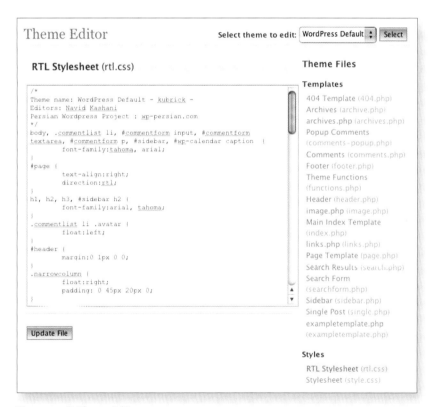

Figure 11.28 Theme Editor.

Theme Editor is a glorified text editor that's embedded in the Themes panel, which means that you need an Internet connection to use it, like anything else in the WordPress administrative interface. Just select the file you want to edit in the list on the right side of the window, or choose it from the Select Theme to Edit drop-down menu. Either way, the file loads in Theme Editor.

Viewing and editing the theme's code

The next step is looking for the code you want to change.

Suppose that you want to remove the gray box from the Author's Grid theme, which I mention at the start of "Customizing the Current Theme" earlier in this chapter, and replace it with a picture. This box is a secondary column, and secondary columns of a theme are called sidebars, so it stands to reason that the box you want to fiddle with is in the file called sidebar.php.

For this example, select sidebar.php in the Theme Editor window. You see this code on the left side of the window:

```
<div class="mpu">
  </div><!--/300x250mpu-->
```

Thanks to some great comments by the theme's builder, it looks as though the gray box is 300 pixels by 250 pixels, which means that you need to replace it with a picture of the same dimensions. You can double-check by looking at this theme's CSS. Select the CSS file to display the code in Theme Editor, and look for the mpu class:

```
.mpu {
  width: 300px;
  height: 250px;
  background: #e5e5e5;
  margin-bottom: 20px;
}
```

That clinches it: Your image should be 300 pixels wide and 250 pixels high to fill that entire box.

Because you know that the box is defined in sidebar.php, select that file in Theme Editor once more to display its code. Then add the boldface code below, substituting your own URL, theme, and photo file name:

```
<div class="mpu">
    <img src="http://www.wordpressforall.com/wordpress/wp-content/
    themes/author-grid/images/scotthead.jpg" alt="scott">
    </div><!--/300x250mpu-->
```

Figure 11.29 shows an example of the result, which has a much better picture in the sidebar, wouldn't you say?

Figure 11.29 Ahhh—this picture is much better than that boring old box. I wonder who the handsome man is.

Most minor changes require some basic HTML knowledge, but you should feel comfortable poking around in any of the files that make up a theme. Just be sure to back up any files that you plan to change so you can recover quickly from any mistakes.

note   Because you're changing the actual files that make up the theme, be sure to back up your customized theme before you make any sort of change. Your changes aren't stored in a WordPress database but in the files themselves, so when you upload a new version of the directory to your Web host, you'll overwrite your custom copy unless you plan ahead.

12

Themes: To Find or to Build?

Lots of people around the world use WordPress and love making themes for it. Best of all, lots of those fine folks want to share their themes with everyone, for free. That's right—you'll find a very healthy freeware market for themes.

In this chapter, I give you the lowdown on finding just the right theme on the Web and on customizing a stock theme to make it your own.

Finding a WordPress Theme

The best place to find a theme for your blog is the WordPress Theme Directory (http://wordpress.org/extend/themes/). This directory is run by the same people who control WordPress itself, and they've set up some ground rules that a theme has to follow to be listed.

Here are some of the requirements:

- All the theme files must be included in a single .zip file. This requirement makes it much easier for you to unzip the theme in a directory and then upload that directory to your WordPress installation.

- The theme must include a file called screenshot.png. If you've read Chapter 11, you may remember that this picture is displayed in the Theme panel of WordPress (which you open by choosing Design > Themes). A theme must have this file to be listed in the Theme Directory, and the file must be a screen shot of the theme in action—not just an icon.

- The theme has to support avatars/gravatars and widgets. (Automattic, the company behind WordPress.com, provides both features and has an interest in seeing them widely adopted. Also, widgets are useful, and avatars are fun.)

- The theme must contain no hidden or sponsored links.

These requirements benefit WordPress theme consumers. They also make the WordPress Theme Directory the best place to find free themes for your blog.

Searching the Theme Directory

Given that the Theme Directory is best of breed for free themes, in this section I show you how you can find themes there.

The directory is searchable, so if you're looking for a three-column theme, you could search for *three columns*. Also, all the themes are tagged by the developers who created them, so looking through the directory's Tags page (http://wordpress.org/extend/themes/tags/) is a great way to see what terms are popular and to get a sense for how themes are described.

The themes are divided into four categories:

- **Featured Themes.** These themes, featured prominently on the front page of the Theme Directory, are handpicked by the directory's editors and usually are at the forefront of theme trends.

- **Most Popular.** The directory tracks download statistics for each theme it contains and highlights those that are being downloaded most often.

- **Newest Themes.** This section is a chronological listing of the newest themes added to the directory.

- **Recently Updated.** These themes aren't the newest but have been changed recently.

Downloading a theme

When you find a theme you're interested in, click its name to see more information about it (**Figure 12.1**), such as how it's tagged and what its user ratings are. You can also click the Author link to find other themes by the same person.

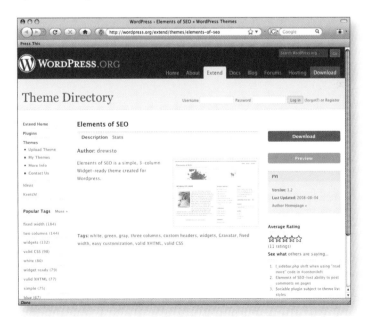

Figure 12.1 Expanded information about the Elements of SEO theme.

The right side of the theme-detail page features a large red Download button, as well as some version information and the date when the theme was last updated. The coolest feature of this page, though, has to be the green Preview button. Clicking that button loads some dummy content into the theme so that you can see what the theme looks like in your browser of choice. You can click around in this demo blog and see all the features of the theme in action—a great way to get a feel for the theme and see whether it's what you're looking for.

Checking out other theme sites

The official WordPress Theme Directory isn't the only place to find a great theme for free. Here are just two of the many other Web sites you can check:

- **NattyWP** (www.nattywp.com) is the home of some very nice, simple themes that are geared to business blogs. The site also offers some premium themes for sale.

- **WordPress Themes** (www.wpthemespot.com) highlights interesting and unique themes from across the Web. The site doesn't have as broad a collection of themes as some other sites do, but I think the quality of the themes highlighted here is pretty high.

Tweaking a Stock Theme

Creating your own theme from scratch is beyond what 98 percent of WordPress users will ever need to do, which is why I recommend just finding a stock theme that you like. The idea is to take a theme that you've downloaded and change certain parts of it—add a field here, take something away there—to make that theme your very own.

In this section, I show you how to change a few features of the default WordPress theme to make it more your own by altering the templates that make up the theme. I'm a fan of showing the author of a post along with the post date and title, for example, but as you see in **Figure 12.2**, WordPress doesn't display the author name by default. You may find it useful to display author names, though, especially if you have a multiple-author blog. To add this information to your blog, you have to open the index.php file and delve into some code.

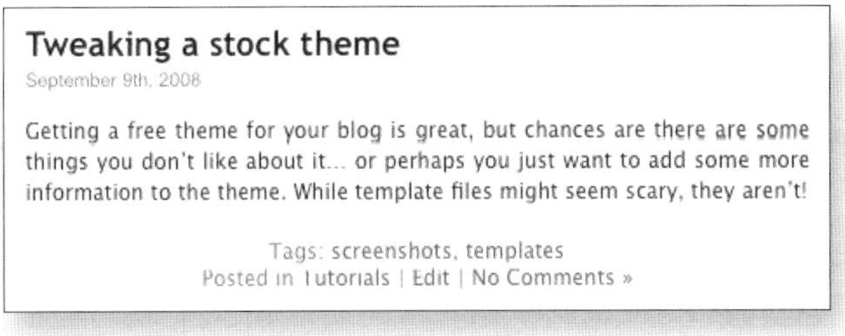

Tweaking a stock theme

September 9th, 2008

Getting a free theme for your blog is great, but chances are there are some things you don't like about it... or perhaps you just want to add some more information to the theme. While template files might seem scary, they aren't!

Tags: screenshots, templates
Posted in Tutorials | Edit | No Comments »

Figure 12.2 A post displayed in the default WordPress theme with the default settings.

Getting into The Loop

Before you dive headfirst into the theme's code, you need to understand a little bit about the workings of template code, which powers every WordPress theme.

WordPress templates use special template tags that retrieve information about your WordPress installation, such as the blog's name or a list of posts. The most critical part of the index.php template file is *The Loop*. This piece of code is the engine that powers much of WordPress.

To view The Loop, open the index.php file of the default theme, which is located in *wordpress*/themes/default (where *wordpress* is your WordPress directory).

have_posts

The Loop starts this way:

```
<?php if (have_posts()) : ?>
    <?php while (have_posts()) : the_post(); ?>
```

The first part, `<?php`, is just standard PHP code that isn't specific to WordPress. The `if (have_posts())` part is a function that queries your WordPress database to see whether you have any posts. If you do, it starts a `while` loop that iterates through each of your posts. Code is executed for each post in The Loop via several template tags, some of which work only within The Loop.

The code in the Loop that is responsible for displaying your posts looks like this:

```
<div class="post" id="post-<?php the_ID(); ?>">
   <h2><a href="<?php the_permalink() ?>" rel="bookmark"
   title="Permanent Link to <?php the_title_attribute();
   ?>"><?php the_title(); ?></a></h2>

<small><?php the_time('F jS, Y') ?> <!-- by <?php the_author()
   ?> --></small>

     <div class="entry">
        <?php the_content('Read the rest of this entry &raquo;');
   ?>
      </div>

<p class="postmetadata"><?php the_tags('Tags: ', ', ', '<br
   />'); ?> Posted in <?php the_category(', ') ?> | <?php edit_
   post_link('Edit', '', ' | '); ?> <?php comments_popup_link('No
   Comments &#187;', '1 Comment &#187;', '% Comments &#187;');
   ?></p>

</div>
```

This code may look intimidating, but when you know what's going on, it isn't scary at all. Most of this code is page-formatting directions, so you can ignore it. The interesting parts are the WordPress tags, because they allow you to display information from your blog. The first template tag is the_ID(), which queries the database and returns the POST_ID for use in the div tag that contains the post.

title

The next section builds the title of the post. All the WordPress magic happens between a pair of <h2> tags that make the title stand out. The tag called the_permalink() returns the permalink of the post. This permalink tag is used in conjunction with the_title_attribute (which returns a clean version of the title by stripping out any HTML code that may be used in the title) and the_title (which returns the title of the post as it was entered) to create the title link. If you want to add *Title:* before each of your blog post titles, the code would look like this:

```
<h2><a href="<?php the_permalink() ?>" rel="bookmark"
  title="Permanent Link to <?php the_title_attribute();
  ?>">Title: <?php the_title(); ?></a></h2>
```

Save the index.php file and reload your blog's home page, and you'll see *Title:* in each post's title (**Figure 12.3**). If you click the permalink and go to the post's page, however, you'll notice that *Title:* is missing. The reason: Individual post pages use a different template (single.php).

Title: Tweaking a stock theme

September 9th, 2008

Getting a free theme for your blog is great, but chances are there are some things you don't like about it… or perhaps you just want to add some more information to the theme. While template files might seem scary, they aren't!

Tags: screenshots, templates
Posted in Tutorials | Edit | No Comments »

Figure 12.3 The first fruits of theme tweaking: an addition to a post title. Useless? Perhaps, but the exercise is instructive.

note If you want the changes you've made in the index.php file to show up on individual post pages, you have to edit that template separately. The single.php file uses the same tags as index.php, so editing it should be a piece of cake.

the_time

The next line is what you're looking for. This line is responsible for the small text below the post title that displays the date when the post was published. Notice that this tag, `the_time()`, takes arguments. By default, `the_time` shows the date in whatever format you set for your blog (by choosing Settings > Date Format). You can also pass along custom formats to this tag by using arguments.

If you want to show the time of the post in addition to the date, for example, use this code:

```
<?php the_time('g:i a') ?> on <?php the_time('F jS, Y') ?>
```

The time tag can show either the time or the date, but not both, so you have to use it twice to show the date in the desired format (**Figure 12.4**).

Title: Tweaking a stock theme
11.17 pm on September 9th, 2008

Figure 12.4 The date and time have been changed to show a little more information.

tip   Check Chapter 5 for some common date formats that you can use with this tag.

the_author

In the same line as the time tag, you'll notice this code:

```
<!-- by <?php the_author() ?> -->
```

The tag called the_author returns the name of the post's author. Why isn't that name showing up on the page, even though the tag is present? That tag has been commented out. The characters <!- -> are *comment tags,* which tell PHP to ignore any code between them. Just delete that comment code, which will make that line look like this:

```
by <?php the_author() ?>
```

The author's name appears as if by magic (**Figure 12.5**).

Title: Tweaking a stock theme
11.17 pm on September 9th, 2008 by scott

Figure 12.5 The post author's user name added to the post.

note   This tag displays the author's login name, which may not be his actual name.

If the user provided his first and last names in his profile, you can tweak the code as follows to displays the author's full name:

```
<?php the_author_firstname(); ?>   <?php the_author_lastname(); ?>
```

Ah—much better (**Figure 12.6**).

Title: Tweaking a stock theme
11.17 pm on September 9th, 2008 by Scott McNulty

Figure 12.6 A user name is nice, but a full name is even better.

the_content

The meat of any blog is the posts, which this bit of code handles:

```
<div class="entry">
  <?php the_content('Read the rest of this entry &raquo;'); ?>
</div>
```

The tag titled `the_content` displays the content (imagine that) of a given post. Notice that this tag takes an argument as well. If you've read Chapter 6, you may recall that you can split a post into two segments by using the `<!--more-->` quicktag. The text you provide in this tag is the text that WordPress uses for the link to the rest of the post. If you want the link to say *Keep reading . . .*, change this code as follows:

```
<?php the_content('Keep reading . . .'); ?>
```

Figure 12.7 shows the result.

Title: Tweaking a stock theme

11.17 pm on September 9th, 2008 by Scott McNulty

Getting a free theme for your blog is great, but chances are there are some things you don't like about it... or perhaps you just want to add some more information to the theme. While template files might seem scary, they aren't!

Keep reading...

Figure 12.7 New text for a link.

note You can enter any text as an argument for the content tag (*the_content*).

Final section (tags, categories, edit link, comments)

The final bit of code in The Loop handles the display of tags and categories, the edit link (if you're logged in), and comments:

```
<p class="postmetadata"><?php the_tags('Tags: ', ', ', '<br
/>'); ?> Posted in <?php the_category(', ') ?> | <?php edit_
post_link('Edit', '', ' | '); ?> <?php comments_popup_link('No
Comments &#187;', '1 Comment &#187;', '% Comments &#187;');
?></p>

</div>
```

As you might expect, the tags titled `the_tags` and `the_category` query the database and return the tags and categories, respectively, that are assigned to this post.

The tag titled `the_tags` has a few more options than its counterpart tag, `the_category`. The first argument is anything you want to show up before the tags appear—perhaps a label (such as *Tags:*), an opening set of HTML tags (such as `<ul><li>`), or a combination of both.

Suppose that you want to display tags as an unordered (bulleted) list preceded by the words *This post tagged with:*. The code you'd use looks like this:

```php
<?php the_tags('This post tagged with: <ul><li>', '</li><li>',
'</li></ul><br />'); ?>
```

Figure 12.8 shows the result.

This post tagged with:

- about
- example
- permalinks

Figure 12.8 You can control how tags are displayed in your posts. Here, the tags appear in an unordered list.

The template tag `the_category` is a little more straightforward. The first argument sets the separator for the categories; the default is a comma followed by a space. You can supply more one more argument to this tag to display parent and subcategories. By default, the tag displays categories in single mode (with the `'single'` argument), meaning that if a post is in a subcategory, WordPress displays only the subcategory. If you change the argument as follows, however, both parent categories and subcategories are displayed (**Figure 12.9**):

```php
<?php the_category(', ', 'multiple') ?>
```

Posted in Book News, Tutorials, WordPress

Figure 12.9 Use the `'multiple'` argument for the category tag to display both parent categories and subcategories assigned to a post.

The template tag `edit_post_link` is an interesting one because most visitors to your blog never see it or interact with it. This tag displays an Edit link on posts when the person visiting your blog is logged in and has sufficient privileges to edit posts (**Figure 12.10**). If both of those conditions aren't met, `edit_post_link` displays nothing. (For more information on editing and other user privileges, flip to Chapter 3.)

Figure 12.10 The Edit link is visible only to users who are logged in and have permission to edit the post they're viewing.

The first argument of the tag is the text of the link; the second argument is anything you want to appear before the link; and the third argument is anything you want to appear after the link. If you want the Edit link to read *ZAP!* instead, that's easy enough to do. Change the tag to read this way:

```php
<?php edit_post_link('ZAP!', '*', '*'); ?>
```

Figure 12.11 shows the result.

ZAP! 2 Comments »

Figure 12.11 You can change the text of the Edit link to whatever you want. (I think *ZAP!* is kind of catchy.)

Rounding out the tags that make up a post is `comments_popup_link`. This tag takes care of displaying a few comment scenarios. Here's an example:

```php
<?php comments_popup_link('No Comments &#187;', '1 Comment
  &#187;', '% Comments &#187;'); ?>
```

This tag tells WordPress to display *No Comments* if the post has no comments; *1 Comment* if the post has one comment; and *Comments* followed by the number of comments if the post has multiple comments. (The % symbol is a variable that stands for the actual comment number.) To change the way that the link reads, simply change the text in the tag.

Right after the comment tag, you see this code (in the default WordPress theme):

```php
<?php endwhile; ?>
```

That's the end of The Loop. Everything after this point won't be repeated for each post in your database.

Closing index.php

The main index.php file is rounded out by the tag team of `next_posts_link` and `previous_posts_link`, both of which are template tags that let readers navigate the archives of your blog. Both tags commonly take one argument that sets the text for the link. The default theme labels the links *Older Entries* and *Newer Entries*.

The Loop may be over, but the index.php file isn't. A PHP `else` statement goes along with this code from earlier in the index.php file:

```
<?php if (have_posts()) : ?>
```

As you may recall from the "have_posts" section earlier in this chapter, this `if` statement checks to see whether you have any posts in your database; if you do, The Loop is called into action, and all the tags I cover in the preceding section display your content. If you don't have any posts in your database, WordPress skips to this section and displays the message *Sorry, but you are looking for something that isn't here*—which I think would make a ton more sense if it said something along the lines of *I haven't started posting yet, but stay tuned!* (If you agree with me, simply change the text and save the index.php file.)

The index.php file ends with this code:

```
<?php get_sidebar(); ?>
<?php get_footer(); ?>
```

The `get_sidebar` tag calls the sidebar code, and the `get_footer` tag adds the footer at the end of the page.

Touching Base with Template Tags

Template tags are very powerful things in WordPress, and this section just scratches the surface of what you can do with them. That being said, most of the time all you'll need to do is change some wording in a tag argument here and there.

To find out more about all the great things you can do with tags, check out the WordPress Codex's Template Tags page:

http://codex.wordpress.org/Template_Tags/

13

Using Plug-Ins

Plug-ins extend what WordPress can do by adding new functionality and features with minimal effort on your part. A dizzying array of plug-ins, both paid and free, is available for WordPress. In fact, for many people, this extensive selection of plug-ins is why they choose WordPress over other blogging tools.

What the heck is a *plug-in?* It's a file (or several files, depending on how complicated the plug-in is) that you upload to your blog.

To see the default plug-ins in your WordPress installation, click the Plugins link in the navigation bar of the WordPress administration inter-face. WordPress opens the Plugin Management panel (**Figure 13.1**), which displays the currently installed plug-ins. An *installed plug-in* is one that has been uploaded and saved in *wordpress*/wp-content/plugins (where *wordpress* is your WordPress installation folder).

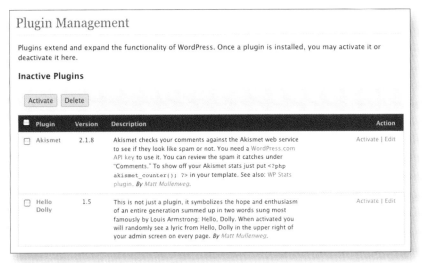

Plugin Management

Plugins extend and expand the functionality of WordPress. Once a plugin is installed, you may activate it or deactivate it here.

Inactive Plugins

[Activate]   [Delete]

☐ Plugin	Version	Description	Action
☐ Akismet	2.1.8	Akismet checks your comments against the Akismet web service to see if they look like spam or not. You need a WordPress.com API key to use it. You can review the spam it catches under "Comments." To show off your Akismet stats just put <?php akismet_counter(); ?> in your template. See also: WP Stats plugin. *By Matt Mullenweg.*	Activate | Edit
☐ Hello Dolly	1.5	This is not just a plugin, it symbolizes the hope and enthusiasm of an entire generation summed up in two words sung most famously by Louis Armstrong: Hello, Dolly. When activated you will randomly see a lyric from Hello, Dolly in the upper right of your admin screen on every page. *By Matt Mullenweg.*	Activate | Edit

Figure 13.1 The Plugin Management panel looks like the long-lost cousin of the Manage Pages and Manage Posts panels.

In WordPress, two plug-ins are installed by default: Akismet and some-thing called Hello Dolly (hello.php). Just having them installed isn't enough, though. To use a plug-in, you have to activate it—as I show you later in this chapter.

tip

In fact, you won't even see Akismet in the Plugin Management panel until you activate it. For details on Akismet, see Chapter 10.

Managing Plug-Ins

Managing plug-ins begins with seeing which plug-ins are active and which are inactive. In a fresh WordPress installation, you have only inactive plug-ins, so the Plugin Management panel contains only the Inactive Plugins section (**Figure 13.2**).

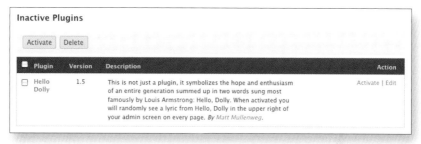

Figure 13.2 The Inactive Plugins section gives you a good amount of information about installed but inactive plug-ins.

WordPress displays information about these plug-ins in four columns:

- **Plugin.** The Plugin column lists plug-ins in alphabetical order; their names are links to more information about them.

- **Version.** The Version column displays the installed version of the plug-in. As with any piece of software, it's important to keep your plug-ins up to date—a task that WordPress can help you with (see "Updating a plug-in" later in this chapter).

- **Description.** The Description column tells you what the plug-in does and who wrote it.

  Hello Dolly (refer to Figure 13.2), for example, doesn't do anything especially useful, but having a line from the musical *Hello, Dolly* displayed on your admin pages can't be a bad thing. (I may be biased, though: I grew up in Yonkers, New York, where most of the action in *Hello, Dolly* takes place.)

- **Action.** This column lists actions that you can perform on each plug-in, such as Activate or Edit. These actions change depending on the state the plug-in is in.

Activating a plug-in

To use a plug-in, you have to activate it. You can accomplish this task in either of two ways:

- Click the check box of the plug-in you want to activate (or select multiple check boxes to activate multiple plug-ins at the same time) and click the Activate button at the top of the Inactive Plugins section (**Figure 13.3**).

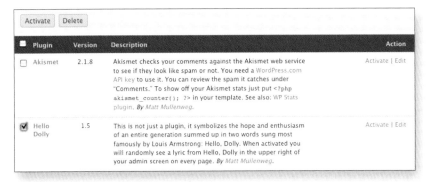

Figure 13.3 Selecting a plug-in to activate.

- Click the Activate link in the plug-in's Actions column. This method works on only one plug-in at a time.

No matter which method you use, WordPress displays a little notice that your plug-in has been activated. It also displays a new Currently Active Plugins section in the Plugin Management panel (**Figure 13.4**). This new section is displayed first in the panel now, followed by the Inactive Plugins section. Also, active plug-ins are displayed with a green background, which makes it easier to tell at a glance which plug-ins are active.

Several things may happen after you activate a plug-in. Hello Dolly is simple and doesn't add any menu items; all it does is display a lyric from the musical on your admin pages (**Figure 13.5**). The Akismet plug-in, on the other hand, adds a menu item to the Plugin Management panel; I cover it in detail in Chapter 10.

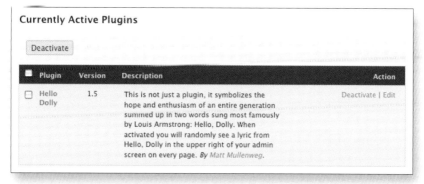

Figure 13.4 Hello Dolly is activated.

Figure 13.5 The words in the top-right corner are lyrics from *Hello, Dolly*. The plug-in works!

Editing a plug-in

Like WordPress itself, plug-ins consist of files—text files, in this case, which you can edit. You can access the editing tools in either of two ways:

- Click the Edit link in the plug-in's Action column (refer to "Managing Plug-Ins" earlier in this chapter).

- Click the Plugin Editor link in the Plugin Management panel's navigation bar.

Either action opens the Plugin Editor panel (**Figure 13.6** on the next page). Much like Theme Editor (refer to Chapter 11), this panel allows you to edit the files that make up your installed plug-ins.

The scrolling pane on the left side of the panel displays the code of the file that's selected on the right side of the panel. If you click the Edit link for a particular plug-in, the Plugin Editor loads that file. The header gives you some information about the file you're editing, including its directory, its name, and its status (active or inactive).

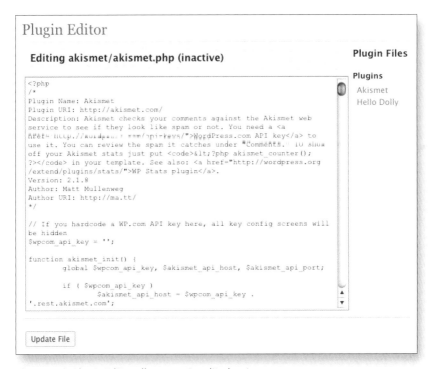

Plugin Editor

Editing akismet/akismet.php (inactive)

Plugin Files

Plugins
Akismet
Hello Dolly

```
<?php
/*
Plugin Name: Akismet
Plugin URI: http://akismet.com/
Description: Akismet checks your comments against the Akismet web
service to see if they look like spam or not. You need a <a
href= http://wordp..... .com/api-keys/">WordPress.com API key</a> to
use it. You can review the spam it catches under "Comments. To show
off your Akismet stats just put <code>&lt;?php akismet_counter();
?></code> in your template. See also: <a href="http://wordpress.org
/extend/plugins/stats/">WP Stats plugin</a>.
Version: 2.1.8
Author: Matt Mullenweg
Author URI: http://ma.tt/
*/

// If you hardcode a WP.com API key here, all key config screens will
be hidden
$wpcom_api_key = '';

function akismet_init() {
        global $wpcom_api_key, $akismet_api_host, $akismet_api_port;

        if ( $wpcom_api_key )
                $akismet_api_host = $wpcom_api_key .
'.rest.akismet.com';
```

Update File

Figure 13.6 Plugin Editor allows you to edit plug-ins.

The right side of the panel lists all the plug-in files that are available for editing. Click the name of a plug-in to load its code into the pane on the left side of the panel. You can simply look at the code and read the comments or change anything you want. If you make any edits (be sure that you know what you're doing!), click the Update File button to save your changes.

note   Be careful while editing a plug-in. Changing or deleting code can have unintended consequences, even though reinstalling a plug-in is fairly easy.

Updating a plug-in

Just like all other software developers, plug-in authors continually change and update their products. Keeping your plug-ins up to date used to be a manual process, but nowadays, WordPress keeps track of your plug-ins and alerts you when an update is available. A small speech-bubble number in the top-right corner of the Plugin Management panel indicates how many plug-ins have available updates (**Figure 13.7**).

Figure 13.7 WordPress alerts you that seven plug-ins need updates.

Click this number to see information about the updates (**Figure 13.8**).

Figure 13.8 Details on available updates.

tip

Pay attention to what versions of WordPress a plug-in supports, especially when a new version of WordPress is released. Sometimes plug-ins need to be updated to play nicely with WordPress changes.

WordPress gives you two options for updating a plug-in:

- Click the Download Version x.x Here link to download the new version of the plug-in and install it at your leisure.

- Click the Upgrade Automatically link to download the update, decompress it, remove the old plug-in, and install the new one.

note

You may not want to use the automatic-upgrade method if you want to check out the new features of a plug-in update before you install it.

Deactivating a plug-in

If you can activate a plug-in, it stands to reason that you can deactivate it as well. Deactivating a plug-in doesn't uninstall it; rather, deactivating it tells WordPress not to load the plug-in's extensions. The features of a deactivated plug-in are no longer accessible via the administration interface.

You have two ways to deactivate a plug-in:

- In the Currently Active Plugins section, click the check box of the plug-in you want to deactivate (or click multiple check boxes to deactivate multiple plug-ins at the same time) and then click the Deactivate button at the top of the section.

- Click the Deactivate link in the plug-in's Action column. This method works on only one plug-in at a time.

When you deactivate a plug-in, another new section appears in the Plugin Management panel: Recently Active Plugins (**Figure 13.9**).

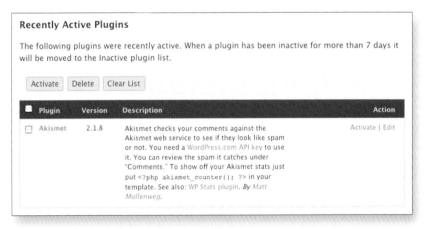

Figure 13.9 The Recently Active Plugins section.

A deactivated plug-in is listed in this section for 7 days before it returns to the Inactive Plugins section, so you can see what plug-ins you used recently and reactive them if you want (using the methods in "Activating a plug-in" earlier in this chapter). If you want to clear this display, click the Clear List button; all the plug-ins listed as Recently Active Plugins immediately move to the Inactive Plugins section.

Deleting a plug-in

Plug-ins are so easy to install, I'm willing to bet that you'll soon have a large number of them cluttering your blog. Sure, you can deactivate plug-ins when you're done with them, but what if you decide that you don't want a certain plug-in installed in your blog at all?

Deleting a plug-in is just as easy as installing one, and you can do it in either of two ways. I describe both methods in the following sections.

Using the Plugin Management panel

In either the Inactive Plugins or Recently Active Plugins section, check the check boxes of the plug-ins that you want to delete; then click the Delete button. WordPress displays the Delete Plugin(s) dialog box (**Figure 13.10**).

Figure 13.10 WordPress knows that people sometimes click Delete by accident, so it asks you to confirm your action.

WordPress wants to make sure that you really want to delete the plug-in, because no undo option is available. You can see all the files associated with this plug-in by clicking the link titled Click to View Entire List of Files Which Will Be Deleted.

When you're sure what you want to do, click Yes, Delete These Files to delete the plug-in, or click No, Return Me to the Plugin List if you have a last-minute change of heart.

Using an FTP program

If you prefer, you can use your FTP program of choice to navigate to the wp-content/plugins directory and delete the folder containing the files for the plug-in you want to remove. The beauty of this method is that it works even when WordPress isn't able to delete the plug-in for some reason.

Finding Plug-Ins

Just as the best place to find themes is the WordPress Theme Directory, the best place to find plug-ins is the official WordPress Plugin Directory (http://wordpress.org/extend/plugins/). This page is your one-stop shop for all WordPress-related plug-ins (well, most of them anyway).

The plug-in directory has three sections:

- Most Popular

- Newest Plugins

- Recently Updated

You can also search for a particular plug-in by name or by a subject if you want your WordPress blog to do something but aren't sure whether a plug-in is available to handle the job.

Each plug-in entry lists a bevy of information about the plug-in: description, installation instructions, frequently asked questions, screen shots, and stats (how often this particular plug-in has been downloaded). Some plug-ins also have an information link.

In the right column, below the orange Download button, is even more information about the plug-in (**Figure 13.11**), including the version number and a link to previous versions (if any).

 Pay close attention to the version of WordPress that the plug-in requires and what it's compatible with. If the version of WordPress you're running falls outside those boundaries, you shouldn't install the plug-in.

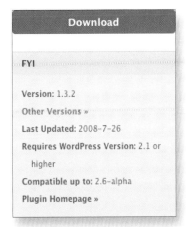

Figure 13.11 Lots of information is listed on the right side of the plug-in's page.

Creating a Plug-In of Your Very Own

Plug-ins can get pretty complicated, requiring knowledge of PHP that goes beyond the scope of this book. But if you want to create your own plug-ins, you should be aware of a formatting issue: If you want your custom plug-in's name, version number, and description to show up in the Plugin Management panel, you need to include some important header information in a PHP comment (PHP comments start with /* and end with */).

Here is an example plug-in that does nothing other than show up correctly in the Plugin Management panel:

```
<?php
/*
Plugin Name: My totally awesome plug-in
Plugin URI: http://www.wordpressforall.com/
Description: This plug-in is only for demonstration purposes
    related to the blog <a href="http://www.wordpressforall.
    com/">WordPress For All</a>.
Author: Scott McNulty
Author URI: http://blog.blankbaby.com/
Version: 1.0
*/

?>
```

Plug-ins are written in PHP, which means you have to open the <php> tag first to let the server know how to handle this file. The rest of the code provides WordPress information to display in the Plugin Management panel. Here's a breakdown of the elements of this code:

- **Plugin Name.** This variable sets the display name of the plug-in— in this case, *My totally awesome plug-in*. That name will be displayed in the name column of each plug-in table.

 note The names of the files that make up your plug-ins don't matter to WordPress, so you can name them whatever you like, but the best practice is to follow a naming convention of some kind.

- **Plugin URI.** This variable is a Web site that contains more informa-tion about your plug-in. The name of your plug-in is a link to this site.

- **Description.** This variable describes your plug-in. Make sure that the description gives people who download your plug-in a good idea of what the plug-in actually does. You can use HTML in this description, so you can link to Web sites that may give the user more information.

- **Author.** You should get credit for all your hard plug-in coding, right? Good thing you do! Simply add your name to this section of the header, and WordPress will credit the plug-in to you.

- **Author URI.** This variable is a link to your Web site, using the Author entry as the text of the link.

- **Version.** For this variable, enter the version number of your plug-in.

Close the comments and then enter the PHP code that makes your plug-in do something. (This example plug-in doesn't do anything.) Finally, close the PHP tag. **Figure 13.12** shows the result.

Figure 13.12 This demonstration plug-in doesn't do anything other than set the proper information for display.

Plug-Ins No Blog Should Be Without

Countless plug-ins are available for WordPress, and all those choices can be a little overwhelming. I'm going to give you a list of five plug-ins that I install in every WordPress blog that I run. I'm not associated with the developers of these plug-ins, all of which are free (though many of the developers accept donations). I just find these plug-ins to be the best of breed, and I can't imagine using WordPress without them.

Here are my top five WordPress plug-ins, in no particular order:

Wordpress [sic] Automatic Upgrade

http://wordpress.org/extend/plugins/wordpress-automatic-upgrade/

WordPress is updated fairly regularly, and though the upgrade process isn't onerous, it can be time consuming (especially if you're running more than one WordPress blog). This plug-in automates the process. It alerts you that an update is available for WordPress, backs up your blog, downloads the latest WordPress version, and installs everything automatically. (If you want a little more control of the process, you can work through each of the five steps manually.)

podPress

http://wordpress.org/extend/plugins/podpress/

If you plan on having a podcast, you need to get podPress. This great plug-in makes podcasting ridiculously easy, embedding the media files for you, helping you get your podcast into podcasting directories, and generally making your life as a podcaster much smoother. A premium (read: paid) version adds some features, but most people will be happy with the free version.

WP-DB-Backup

http://wordpress.org/extend/plugins/wp-db-backup/

Backing up your blog's database is very important. That's where all your content is stored, and if you ever have a problem with your database, you'll be bummed if you didn't back up on a regular basis. WP-DB-Backup makes it super-easy to back up your WordPress tables, as well as any other tables in your WordPress database. You can also set the plug-in to schedule backups and to e-mail the backup files to you.

continues on next page

Plug-Ins No Blog Should Be Without *continued*

Bad Behavior

http://wordpress.org/extend/plugins/bad-behavior/

Akismet (see Chapter 10) fights comment spam by cataloging various identifying marks and then sending comments that have those marks to the spam queue. Bad Behavior stops the bots that leave comment spam from leaving the spam in the first place.

WP Security Scan

http://wordpress.org/extend/plugins/wp-security-scan/

I know what you're thinking: "Another lame security related plug-in? I thought blogging was supposed to be fun!" Blogging *is* fun, but the popularity of WordPress has made it a big target for hackers. Security Scan looks at various settings (both for WordPress and for file permissions) and makes suggestions based on what it finds. I run this scan every time I update WordPress (because I'm paranoid), and it's served me well.

14

Troubleshooting and Maintenance

I've been running WordPress blogs for a long time, and I haven't run into many major issues over the years. This fact speaks to the hard work that faceless coding volunteers do to make WordPress as solid a product as it is. Still, you should know some things to check in the unlikely event that you run into an issue. You can also save yourself a heaping helping of grief by doing some small things to make sure that your copy of WordPress stays a lean, mean blogging machine.

Troubleshooting Problems

Problems always crop up, but all isn't lost when you encounter a problem. Don't panic—in this section, I outline a few simple troubleshooting steps that should get you out of many common jams.

You get an error instead of blog content

The most common issue that you'll encounter in WordPress is trouble with the communications between your installation of WordPress and the database that holds your blog's users, content, and some settings. **Figure 14.1** shows one example: the dreaded "Error establishing a database connection" error.

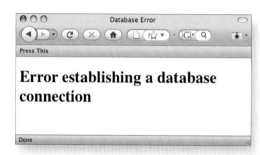

Figure 14.1 An error message alerting you that something's amiss with your database.

If you see an error like this one, your blog can't talk to its database. You can try the following steps in order:

1. Make sure that your database server is up.

   If your database server is down, you can do little to fix this error other than getting the database server back online. WordPress is highly dynamic, meaning that it queries the database to build all pages (both public and admin pages), so without a database, WordPress is fairly useless.

 note You may have to call your Web-hosting company to ask whether this server is down.

2. Try connecting to your database with whatever management tools you use.

   If the database is up and running, the problem is with WordPress.

3. Check your wp-config.php file to make sure that the `DB_NAME`, `DB_USER`, `DB PASSWORD`, and `DB_HOST` parameters all have the proper information.

See Chapter 2 for details on editing your wp-config file.

> **tip** Whenever you change the database user password (for security reasons or what have you), make sure that you update the wp-config file with the proper values.

If the wp-config file shows that all your database information is correct, you should try one last step:

4. Reset the WordPress database user password in both the wp-config file and MySQL.

This step ensures that both passwords are the same and should fix the problem. See Chapter 2 for more information.

You can't log in to WordPress

If you have this problem, chances are that you've just forgotten your password. (It happens to the best of us.)

To solve the problem, follow these steps:

1. Click the Lost Your Password? link below the login form.

WordPress displays a pop-up window (**Figure 14.2**).

Figure 14.2 Enter your username or e-mail address in this window.

2. Enter your user name or your e-mail address in the text box.

 note The e-mail address you enter has to be the one associated with your WordPress account (see Chapter 2).

3. Click the Get New Password button.

WordPress sends an e-mail message to the address you entered in Step 2.

4. Click the link in this e-mail message (**Figure 14.3**) to generate a new password for your account.

WordPress e-mails the new password to you.

Figure 14.3
The e-mail contains a link that allows you to reset your password.

 note If you don't click the link in the e-mail message, your password isn't reset. This feature safeguards against someone locking you out of your own blog by changing your password.

tip If you generate a random password, be sure to change your password to something more memorable after you log in. See Chapter 3 for details.

Your blog has been hacked! OMG!

One downfall of using the most popular blogging software out there is that WordPress blogs are targets for hackers. If you don't keep your WordPress installation current (see "WordPress updates are also your friends" later in this chapter), someone could exploit a known security vulnerability in your blog. I've seen this situation happen to very savvy bloggers, so don't think that it can't happen to you.

Generally, a hacker crafts a bot that trawls the Internet looking for vulnerable installations of WordPress. When it finds a vulnerable blog, the bot exploits the vulnerability to access your blog and insert links to various sites of ill repute. This technique is an effort to use your blog to increase those sites' Google PageRank scores.

 note PageRank is an algorithm that Google uses to assign scores to *all* pages in its index. The higher the score, the better, so getting more links increases a site's PageRank score.

Chances are that if you see several odd links on your blog, you've been hacked. To regain control, follow these steps:

1. Calm down.

   Having your blog hacked sucks, but you could suffer far worse cyber-crimes. (Identity theft tops the list in my book.)

2. Let your Web host know.

   Giving your host notice alerts the company to check its systems (and its other customers' servers).

3. Change your WordPress password.

 tip You shouldn't use the same user name/password combo for your blog that you do for all your other online accounts.

4. Check out the Manage Users page in WordPress, and delete any users that you didn't create—especially any that have Administrator privileges.

   Chapter 3 has all the details on managing users, including the Manage Users page.

5. Log in to your database, using your database management tool of choice; double-check all the users there; and delete any users that you didn't create.

6. Change the database user password, and update the wp-config file (refer to "You get an error instead of blog content" earlier in this chapter).

7. Delete your themes (which have been hacked) and reinstall them.

   Turn to Chapter 11 for directions on installing themes.

8. If you've been very good about backing up your data, completely delete and then reinstall WordPress (see Chapter 2).

   This method is the only way to make sure that all remnants of the hack are erased.

Heading off Trouble Before It Begins

Troubleshooting means that you're in trouble. I'd much rather avoid trouble and get on with the rest of my life (in which I avoid all sorts of other work; it's a skill). You can do a few simple things to your WordPress blog in tip-top shape and avoid trouble in the long run.

Backups are your friends

My list of top five plug-ins in Chapter 13 includes WP-DB-Backup, which backs up your MySQL data automatically. You don't have to do anything (win!). Making backups of your database covers your users and content, but it doesn't cover anything that's in your wp-content directory (see Chapter 2). You'll have to back up your media library, plug-ins, and themes separately.

 note I urge you to make these backups, because by the time you realize that you need a backup, it's too late to start.

Using the Export panel

If you don't want to use that plug-in or need to make a one-off backup of the contents of your blog, choose Manage > Export to open the Export panel (**Figure 14.4**). This panel is where you can export some or all of your blog's content to an XML file.

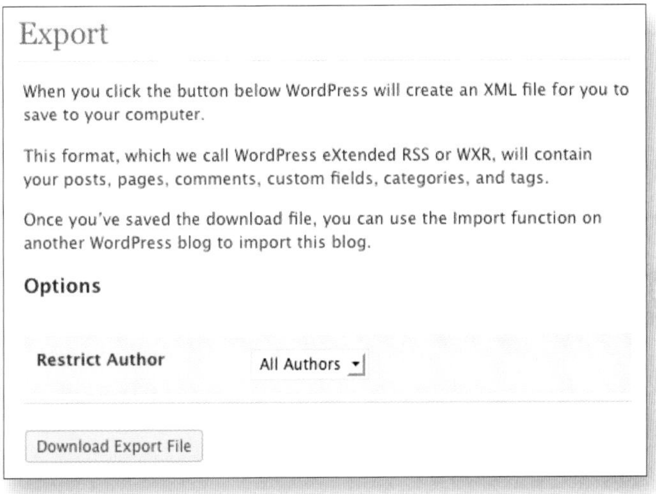

Export

When you click the button below WordPress will create an XML file for you to save to your computer.

This format, which we call WordPress eXtended RSS or WXR, will contain your posts, pages, comments, custom fields, categories, and tags.

Once you've saved the download file, you can use the Import function on another WordPress blog to import this blog.

Options

Restrict Author   All Authors ▾

Download Export File

Figure 14.4 The WordPress Export panel makes it a breeze to export your WordPress content to an XML file.

 note You can export only text from this panel; you still need to back up your files and wp-content folder separately.

Exporting posts by author

One of the nicest things about the WordPress export functionality is that you can choose to export only posts by one author. This feature comes in handy in a multiple-poster blog when one author decides that he wants to strike out on his own. You can give this person a file containing just his posts.

To export a single author's posts, follow these steps:

1. Choose Manage > Export.

   The Export panel opens.

2. From the Restrict Author drop-down menu, choose the author you're interested in.

3. Click the Download Export File button.

   WordPress creates a file of the author's posts.

Importing export files

When you have an export file, you'll probably want to do something with it. To import export files into WordPress, follow these steps:

1. Choose Manage > Import to open the Import panel.

   This panel displays a list of sources from which WordPress can import content, including RSS feeds, other blogging systems, and WordPress backup files.

2. Select WordPress in the list.

   The Import WordPress panel opens.

3. Select your file.

   WordPress imports the content.

When you import from a WordPress backup, you have several options:

- You can map the authors in the file to existing authors in your WordPress blog, or you can have the authors in the import file created automatically in addition to the existing authors (**Figure 14.5**).

- You can have WordPress attempt to download files that are attached to the exported posts (assuming that those files are accessible from their original URLs).

Import WordPress

Assign Authors

To make it easier for you to edit and save the imported posts and drafts, you may want to change the name of the author of the posts. For example, you may want to import all the entries as admins entries.

If a new user is created by WordPress, a password will be randomly generated. Manually change the user's details if necessary.

1. Import author: **scott**
   Create user | scott |
   or map to existing - Select -   ▾|

2. Import author: **admin**
   Create user | admin |
   or map to existing - Select -   ▾|

Import Attachments

☐ Download and import file attachments

(Submit)

Figure 14.5 The Assign Authors page of the Import WordPress panel gives you several import options.

WordPress updates are also your friends

WordPress updates often come at a fast and furious rate, and they can be tough to keep up with. But I strongly urge you to keep your blog as current as possible. Luckily, WordPress alerts you when a new update is available for download.

The point releases are especially important because they're released to address known flaws. (*Point release* is software speak for a release that doesn't add features but focuses on bug and security fixes. It increments the version number by only a point, so WordPress 2.6 becomes WordPress 2.6.1.)

tip   Subscribe to the WordPress Development blog to keep abreast of WordPress news such as updates (http://wordpress.org/development/).

Manual updates

Updating your installation of WordPress is easy, assuming that you have good backups. *Updating* may be something of a misnomer, because you're really just replacing all the WordPress files and running the installation script (which updates your database). You just have to make sure that you back up everything (themes, media, and the like) and upload your backup copies to your newly updated copy of WordPress when you're done.

Automatic updates

A much easier way to update WordPress is to use the Wordpress [sic] Automatic Upgrade plug-in, which I mention in Chapter 13. I can't stress enough how much easier this plug-in makes your life. It backs up your files and your database before it updates your blog, and it maintains any files that you customized. Check it out; you won't be sorry.

The pain of popularity

WordPress generates pages dynamically as people load them. No page is ever out of date; WordPress always displays the information as you have it entered in your database. Update a post, and the very next person who reads that post sees your changes. This feature truly is great.

Well, actually, it's great until a link to your blog gets posted to Digg. Then thousands of people start loading your blog, generating tens of thousands of queries against your database server to generate the same page for each visitor. This sudden upswing in traffic brings down your database, and as you know, WordPress can't display anything without a database. This situation is where the concept of caching comes into play.

Several WordPress plug-ins can help you weather a sudden influx of traffic without having to pony up the money for a beefier Web-hosting contract. I'm a fan of WP Super Cache, myself (http://wordpress.org/extend/plugins/wp-super-cache/).

Caching works on the simple concept that most of the content on your blog doesn't change much, so why create the pages from scratch every time someone visits? Instead, you can keep a premade copy on hand and serve that up to your visitors. This method lessens the impact on the database server, which doesn't need to provide all that information for every page, and it lessens the load on the Web server, which can serve up only static files that don't require processing.

You don't have to wait for your blog to become incredibly popular to install these caching options. Forewarned is forearmed. It's best to prepare your blog for heavy traffic, because you can't always predict what will catch the eyes of the Internet hordes.

 note   **The downside of caching is that if you update a page, it may take a little while for the change to be reflected on your site. Keep this drawback in mind if you update your blog frequently.**

Final Words of Bloggerly Wisdom

You're clearly interested in blogging because you went to the trouble of buying this book (thanks!), so I want to end with a few words about making your blog successful:

- **You are the key.** When you come right down to it, the blogging system you use matters very little to the success of your blog. Sure, you'll be more likely to post if you use a well-designed blogging tool like WordPress, which gets out of your way and helps you concentrate on blogging, but *you* are the key factor in your blog. Your passion, your knowledge, and your viewpoint will make your blog stand out from the rest.

- **Always keep in mind why you're blogging.** Some people blog for fame, some just want to keep in contact with friends, and other simply love to write (that's the group I fall into). The reason why you blog has a big effect on what you blog about and on how you look at blogging decisions. Keep your blogging goal in mind (even if your goal is just to have fun), and given time and attention, your blog should flourish.

- **People judge a book by its cover.** You can admit it—the awesome cover is at least part of the reason you bought this book. People like pretty things. This is true of blogs as well as books. Make sure that your posts are well formatted and include media (when appropriate), and that your blog's theme is pleasing to the eye.

- **Blogging is active, not passive.** The best way to get people reading your blog is to read *their* blogs and interact with them. Leave comments, and link to blog posts you enjoy. After a while, you'll notice that other bloggers are returning the favor, and they'll tell two friends ... who'll tell two friends. You get the idea.

Index

Building a
WORDPRESS
BLOG
People Want to Read

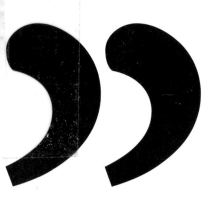

Scott McNulty